DRAWINGS AND DIGRESSIONS

BY

LARRY RIVERS

DRAWINGS AND DIGRESSIONS

BY

LARRY RIVERS

WITH CAROL BRIGHTMAN

Clarkson N. Potter, Inc. / Publishers, New York

DISTRIBUTED BY CROWN PUBLISHERS, INC., NEW YORK

First published 1979 in the United States by Clarkson N. Potter, Inc., a division of Crown Publishers, Inc.

Clarkson N. Potter, Inc.
A division of Crown Publishers, Inc.
One Park Avenue
New York, N.Y. 10016

Published simultaneously in Canada by General Publishing Company Limited.
Printed in Japan by Toppan Printing Co., Inc.

LIBRARY OF CONGRESS CATALOGING IN PUBLICATION DATA

Rivers, Larry, 1923–
   Drawings and digressions.

   1. Rivers, Larry, 1923–   2. New York
School.   I. Brightman, Carol, joint author.
II. Title.
NC139.R56A4   1979   741.9′73   79-4614

ISBN 0-517-53430-4
ISBN 0-517-53779-6 lim. ed.

ACKNOWLEDGMENTS AND PERMISSIONS

Page 24 "A Send-off for Richard Lindner," by Larry Rivers, *Art in America*, Nov.–Dec. 1978.

Page 25 and 35: "Why I Paint as I Do," an interview by Frank O'Hara, *Horizon*, Sept.–Oct. 1959.

Page 60: "If You Can't Draw, Trace," Frank Bowling talks with Larry Rivers, *Arts Magazine*, Feb. 1971.

Page 81: "How to Proceed in the Arts," by Larry Rivers and Frank O'Hara, *Evergreen Review*, July–Aug. 1961.

Page 115: "My Life Among the Stones," by Larry Rivers, *Location*, Spring 1963.

Page 145 and 153: "Larry Rivers," an interview by Gaby Rodgers, *Newsday*, Nov. 12, 1978.

Page 171: "Eulogy for Frank O'Hara," *Homage to Frank O'Hara*, ed. by Bill Berkson and Joe Le Sueur, Big Sky, November 12, 1978. Reprinted with permission.

Page 173: Excerpt from "For the Chinese New Year and Bill Berkson." From *Lunch Poems* by Frank O'Hara, City Lights Books, 1964. Reprinted with permission.

Page 188: Larry Rivers: Dick Cavett Interview, Dec. 26–27, 1977.

CONTENTS

In order not to detract from the play of text and art, data on measurements, media, and owners have been compiled and listed by page number at the back of the book. In general, Mr. Rivers used sketch pads ranging in size from 8″ x 10″ to 14″ x 17″ for his drawings in pencil. Mixed-media works tend to be larger, and the reader is urged to consult the list that begins on page 261 for precise information.

Drawings and Digressions was inspired by the show of Larry Rivers' drawings and works on paper mounted by the Marlborough Gallery in 1977. The works seen as a group emphasized Rivers' lyrical and sensitive qualities—qualities sometimes obscured by the energy and flamboyance of his larger works and paintings. It is this delicacy, sensitivity, and extraordinary way of using the pencil that we hope to bring forward with this book. Drawing is such an integral part of Rivers' work as a whole that we have included a few paintings and multimedia pieces where they were valuable as examples of draftsmanship, as illustration to the text, or as the final work for which the drawings were preliminary stages. This kind of flexibility seemed in keeping with the spirit of the artist and his work.

Rivers was (and is) an extremely prolific artist. He frequently drew the same subject many times and gave the same title to several works; this has led to problems in tracing own-ers. In a few instances where we have been unable to determine ownership, we have credited the works "Private collection." If the owners of these works will write, we will be happy to include more specific credit in forthcoming editions. (Please note that "Private collection" may also denote owners who have requested that their names be withheld.)

This book would not have been possible without the patience and unstinting help of many people. For their assistance and advice in bringing together the photographs for this book, I want to express thanks to Pierre Levai, Dorothy Herman, Vibeke Levy, and especially Anne Milner at the Marlborough Gallery; to the staffs at the Robert Miller Gallery and the ACA Galleries; to Claudia Bismark and Mikki Carpenter, Rights and Reproductions, the Museum of Modern Art; to Alexandra Schwartz, Prints and Illustrated Books, the Museum of Modern Art; to Anselmo Carini, Department of Prints and Drawings, the Art Institute of Chicago; to Doralynn Pines, Photograph Services, the Metropolitan Museum of Art; to Robert Mates who photographed many of the works and to Carol Selle who had many of the works photographed for the 1968 drawing show at the Chicago Institute of Art and generously supplied us with her files; to Amy Simon who helped us trace owners; and finally to all of the other museums, galleries, and private collectors who have given permission to reproduce their works or who have lent them to be photographed.

To those at Clarkson N. Potter, I wish to express my thanks to Ellen Gilbert, Pam Pollack, Elizabeth Ferranti, Michael Fragnito, Nancy Novogrod, Jo Fagan and especially to Jane West and our talented and indispensable designer, Hermann Strohbach.

Finally I wish to thank Larry Rivers and Carol Brightman for their uniquely readable and fascinating manuscript.   C.S.

FOREWORD

"To put it all in a sentence, our strange
artist depicts at the same time the gestures
and attitudes, whether magnificent or grotesque,
of living creatures, and also their brilliant explosion in space."

Baudelaire, *The Painter of Modern Life*

Suddenly this introductory text is long overdue at the publishers, and I'm faced for the first time with really thinking about my gifted and garrulous friend and his work. I've known them both for so long—thirty years, incredibly, or so it seems to me—and I've never thought about them, in the same way that one never *thinks* about the people at the center of one's life—mate or children. They are so close that they are in us; the thinking goes on no doubt, but somewhere under the surface of thought. To wake up, to contemplate them as individuals of the kind one sees on the street, can be a shock.

This isn't to say that Larry and I have been in close association all these years. Sometimes we don't see each other for months, or, as happened when I lived in France, for years. It's one of those friendships that are so well rooted that they don't need to be pursued, polished, tended—the "easy maintenance" kind—and there is an unusual pleasure in such a relationship, a natural-

ness, so that I still feel I am seeing his life and his work from very close up.

I first met Larry in July 1949. I had just graduated from Harvard and had hoped to go to graduate school there, but wasn't accepted. I did get accepted at Columbia, and came to NYC with trepidation, for I had enjoyed the cozy Cambridge atmosphere—"sheep may safely graze," as a pianist friend of mine had once said of it. I didn't feel I was "ready for" the big city (I had grown up in the country and at that point Boston seemed like metropolis enough). Nevertheless, at the encouragement of Kenneth Koch, who had graduated a year ahead of me, had come to New York, and was assuring me that it was an excellent place, I did come and almost immediately, to my surprise, found a job, albeit a fairly menial one in the Brooklyn Public Library. Kenneth introduced me to some of his friends: the painter Jane Freilicher, the poet and playwright Arnold Weinstein, and Larry. (Larry

and Arnold were then sharing a loft on Second Avenue near St. Mark's Place, in the heart of what would one day be the East Village—I don't think it was called that then. That studio was to become an important place in my New York life—the following year Rudy Burckhardt shot his movie *Mounting Tension* there, the penultimate scene of which was an epic brawl between Larry and me during which we were supposed to wreck the place and knock each other unconscious.)

I can just about remember the first time we met. I believe it was at Kenneth's loft on Third Avenue and Sixteenth Street, where Kenneth let me stay until I found a place of my own. (At that time the El was still running, and Kenneth's front windows were at El level, and he would occasionally beguile the time by donning a rubber ape mask and leaning out of the window as the trains went by—that was the summer of *Mighty Joe Young*, a marvelously inept King Kong type movie we had both en-

7

joyed.) I think I was told by Kenneth, or perhaps I figured it out myself when Larry and I met, that he was this special person, someone who was going to be a "famous artist." At that time he was painting in a style strongly influenced by Bonnard—there had been a big and revelatory Bonnard show at the Museum of Modern Art the previous year. In fact, Larry's work was then so derivative that I wondered a bit how he was going to manage becoming famous, yet one knew, somehow, that it would happen. He would work it out. There was that kind of conviction in his voice—a rather disordered kind that one sensed in the frequent abrupt crescendos when he talked, when an idea about art, usually an aside in a conversation on some more frivolous topic, would suggest itself and his voice would rise in the somewhat abrasive but agreeable way it still does, and his face would be transformed by a benevolent animation that it still gets when he wants to tell you something that's just occurred to him that he thinks you'll want to know. There was also the fact that Larry, the ex-Hans Hofmann student, had been singled out by Clement Greenberg, in a review in *The New Republic*, I believe. Greenberg had called him "better than Bonnard," or so the story went. This set the seal on one's notion of Larry as somebody destined to go places, even though he was having trouble paying the rent and his work looked more like a homage to a modern master than that of the innovator he sounded like.

Larry kept the Second Avenue studio but moved his family (mother-in-law, son, and stepson) to a parlor floor apartment in a rather grubby former town house at 77 St. Mark's Place (later on W. H. Auden moved to an apartment on an upper floor of the same building). It was there, I think, that Larry first painted and

drew me. The drawing still exists, though I don't know what became of the painting. At that time, Larry's art already seemed very much an extension of his daily life, as it does today. There were usually a few people—sometimes quite a few—around the apartment while he was working—children, relatives, girl friends, babysitters, fellow artists—and the work would be conducted in the midst of a general cacophony, including consultations with Berdie, his mother-in-law, over that night's supper menu. The strokes got laid down like bursts of talk, sometimes simultaneous with them: that is, Larry would deliver himself of a sudden insight into art or sex while slamming down a line or brushstroke that would find its way into the picture without his help, so intent was he on other matters. Most conversations are dominated by chance, darting from one topic to another even when they seem most deliberate, but it seems that ours, mine and my friends' at the time, were even more disjunct than most, as though we were trying to turn the non sequitur into an art form. And perhaps the rhythm of these exchanges got into the work, for after the Bonnard period Larry's work began to change radically. His subjects would be missing an eye, while the other eye was drawn in with exaggerated care. Or most of the features would be smudged out except for the chin, projecting forward in eerie relief from the veil of the face. Or, rather than letting the whole be deduced from the parts, he would exaggerate everything as he was to do later on in the portraits of Clarice, where facial features and parts of the body are carefully labeled in French.

Erasures were important in his drawing then as they are today. Erasing was very much a thing in the 1950s—we all know about Rauschenberg's erasing of a de Kooning drawing, but of course de Kooning had

been partly obliterating them himself for years, as had Giacometti in France. What did it mean? Perhaps it was an extension of the Impressionists' urge to present nature exactly as the eye perceives it. Even they were unaware of how careless the eye can be, sometimes taking in next to nothing even though it is wide open on the irregularities of the reality of the moment. Hence the need for further drastic reductions. In order to isolate the reality that is real at the moment, much must be whittled away, buried, undrawn. The title of one of Michel Leiris's autobiographical works, Biffures (Erasures) could be the title of Larry's autobiography in his drawings. During all the talking and the drawing we are being led into the artist's life through the back door, or the stage door—*l'entrée des artistes.* The real will emerge only after it's pared down to something that at first looks inessential, inconsequential, then is gradually recognized as the important thing. Someone said that a portrait is a picture of someone in which there's something wrong with the mouth, and Fairfield Porter used to say that to correct that "something" was to kill the portrait. That something "wrong" is, it often seems, precisely what Larry is trying to get at in his portraits—the rest matters less.

Having known him and his work for such a long time I am, as I started out to say, less conscious of its development than an outsider might be. I did notice when his postimpressionist phase quickly developed into a more brash and less lush kind of painting, aware of the abstract expressionists and also of Soutine—MOMA also had a big Soutine show in about 1950. It seems now that those surveys at the Modern (which included Bonnard, Munch, and Matisse) always had immediate repercussions among painters, perhaps because they had seen less art than

Portrait of John Ashbery, 1962

young painters today—travel to Europe wasn't all that common yet and the media hadn't filled in the gaps. Or perhaps young artists today just absorb things differently. This expressionist style soon yielded to the calmer lyricism of the portraits of Berdie and the two boys, and of Frank O'Hara, where Larry seemed to be aiming at a hyperrealism that always eluded him at the last moment—Frank's neck would be too long, or the torso didn't quite fit the legs—and that was its powerful charm. There was an exciting period when Larry was going with a girl named Molly when everything seemed on the verge of flying apart into a rainbow pointillism. And there were big ambitious works of the sixties that incorporated assemblage—

but I'll leave it to Larry to talk about all this. What I wanted to say is that I lived through his phases unreflectingly, as one lives one's own life, when all is said and done, and that the work means more to me for that reason, I think. And perhaps that was the best way to experience what after all has a logic, but a logic of the painter's caprice and of the accidents of the moment—the convincing kind.

No one talks more than Larry, as you'll see from the taped fragments of speech accompanying the illustrations in this book. He is always in the throes of trying to get to the bottom of something, sometimes something important but even more often something trivial. It's a kind of itch, and the drawings go after it—what-

ever it is—in the same way. It's in the delving, gouging, erasing, and the last-ditch restoring of a vital line or shadow. The movement and the process, not what they may manage to come up with, are what matter. The talk also moves by slashing indirection. The drawing and the talking, even at their most idle and indiscreet (there's always a bit of the tragic buffoon, the Papa Karamazov, out to embarrass himself and his entourage—but redemption comes about through embarrassment), go together for me, and make the value of this collection. As a result, these partially drawn, overheard faces seem themselves to have something urgent to communicate to us, the artist and his spectators, once we have finally shut up.

INTRODUCTION

Summer 1977. The great exhibitions of Cézanne, Monet, Seurat, and Matisse had begun to circulate through the national museums. At the *New York Times*, one critic wondered whether "these most exalted of human achievements" should even "be made to hit the road," but in any event, heads were duly bowed. This was High Church. For Larry Rivers, a younger member of the New York School of Art, which began thirty-five years ago in the shadow of the Church, the times might be said to have come full circle. Established names like Jasper Johns, Robert Rauschenberg, and his own—not to mention elders such as de Kooning, Kline, and Rothko—appeared in eclipse, while true reverence seemed to revert like ancestral memories in times of stress, to the masters. No wonder that in August 1977, when I taped the first of ten interviews from which the "digressions" are drawn, Rivers was—and remains—involved with the question of value, of what endures in his work. And his questioning—sometimes funny, sometimes cool, sometimes self-critical, always urgent—is also in a deeper sense an inquiry for an entire generation of artists.

It is not fashionable these days to think in terms of generations. They keep burning out. In the middle sixties, speaking of fame and fortune and the culture boom, Rivers told a critic: "It isn't all that settled yet whether this is going to last. The lights may go out." He was worried then that the demands of the ego would be merciless. "I could not stand to be ignored, perhaps insulted. I might commit suicide." He has survived—as he would say—like we all do. But what of the achievements of that postwar movement of painters, whose assault on established canons of taste stimulated a public debate and popular interest in art which was unprecedented in American culture?

These pictures survive in a kind of half-life on museum and gallery walls, trophies removed from their time and place to entertain a paying public, artifacts whose value in the marketplace depends (as always) on their rarity, their inaccessibility. But look for the signs of life which give birth to this work, and the pulse is weak. All but forgotten is that whirlwind of competing influences: the wartime presence of Mondrian, Léger, Chagall, Ernst, and Lipchitz; collectors and critics looking for a new American art to lift some of the gilt from the French lily; American artists scrambling for new patronage after the collapse of WPA support during the New Deal. There is no surer indication that the lessons of a generation have been lost than when its products are immortalized, while the historical ground from which they came is cut away.

"When we talk about art," Larry Rivers says, "we can't help but talk about its relationship to life." And in *Drawings and Digressions* he leads us from his own work to the human subjects and influences that shaped it; as a result, we begin to retrieve a sense of the era and how it was lived. What Rivers presents are the felt conditions of the artist's struggle—not an elaborate framework of psychological and aesthetic interpretation, but the rough-and-tumble play of ambition, social isolation and romanticism; the role of drugs, sexual politics, envy ("Be ready to admit that jealousy moves you more than art"), as well as loyalty within the charmed circle of the Cedar Bar, and a certain cynicism for the art theories of trend-setting dealers, set beside an aim to please, to make up for lost time as lonely artist. Rivers tracks this struggle down to the present, to the wheeling and dealing and high jinks of the sixties, and its moments of camaraderie as well, and later, to the nervous momentum of career once the honeymoon is over, followed by the apparent willingness of so many to go gentle into the dark night of the seventies.

Larry Rivers, who has always made the world of this generation his chief subject, is one survivor who hasn't let go. In his work the images change with the times. Family, artist-friends, musicians, poet-collaborators and collaborations, venturesome dealers and girl friends from the fifties are succeeded later by patrons and collectors and the commissioned girl friends of collectors, a changing of the guard but still actors in the living drama. Images of the masters, the Renaissance heroics of Rembrandt, the little big men of David and Delacroix, a Gainsborough lady, these images recur again and again like talismans, linking the unbeliever—through the rubric of parody—to some belief in the holding power of tradition. The hinge between art and a certain social reality, and its cult of the masterpiece, remains unbroken.

It is all here in the drawings, assemblages, and paintings, and in the digressions there are the questions and some old quarrels, insults nursed and resolved, or suspended by time,

together with the thoughtful reappraisal of the work of friends and competitors. But no more critical eye is cast than the one Rivers reserves for himself and his work. And how could it be otherwise?

Larry Rivers's whole career is a study in contradiction—frankly acknowledged and tested again and again against the ego's demand for assurance, control, consistency. More often than not the ego goes unappeased. In the artist's search for consistency, nothing flops like success, but the going is rough. In the midst of experiment, in the grip of new mediums, Plexiglas, airbrush, projectors, there is that longing for a steadiness of spirit which Rivers expresses most eloquently in his postmortem for the painter Richard Lindner. In the sway of benevolent tradition, of portraiture on a grand scale, or the excavation of old images ("The Golden Oldies," 1978), there is, on the contrary, a nagging hunger for fresh material which may constitute real art.

It's hard to know whether to give yourself a tinsely atmosphere, Rivers says, or to present yourself as some old master with all the perennial values. If you have both impulses, as does Larry Rivers, the test of a first-rate talent may be the same as Fitzgerald's test for a first-rate intelligence: the ability to hold two contradictory ideas in mind at the same time. At his best, this is exactly what Rivers has done.

In the early fifties, when the new stars of the New York School were rising, and critics like Clement Greenberg and Harold Rosenberg were hailing the efforts of Pollock and de Kooning and Kline to turn the *action* of painting into its own object, there was Larry Rivers possessed by a fantastic desire to draw realistically, to identify with the history of art, to prove himself an artist in the classical sense. Rivers's concern with

subject matter—specifically the subject of his own life and the grand historical myths that haunted it—appeared decidedly arcane. "I felt as if I should be accepted," he recalls of the early years at the Cedar Bar. "I'm an artist and I like big paintings and I appreciated what they [the abstract expressionists] were doing; aspects of their work even crept into my realism, but I wanted different things. I wanted to tell a story." This was more than a question of aesthetics.

Rivers reminds us that by the early fifties the bold stroke and spatter of the postwar American expressionist had suddenly become a kind of international currency. "More and more money went into it, and in some way it really was a part of the emergence of America as a world power. Instead of America looking toward Europe, Europe began to look toward America," he notes, "and we went to ourselves." For a man like Rivers, who by his own reckoning is profoundly moved by outside influences—not least the influence of the fortunate and the famous—the conflict was acute.

Rivers's iconoclasm had deeper, more complex roots. In a postwar art world hungry for new sensations, Larry Rivers arrived as a kind of carrier of cultural norms established over four centuries ago with the rise of oil painting. Certain archetypal conventions of studio art—history-in-costume, the nude study, the "great man"—stripped of their original patina of completeness, to be sure, and like the three Napoleons metamorphosing into *The Greatest Homosexual* (1964), figures in search of form; nonetheless, these were icons from an imperial past hardly less potent in their appeal to the senses than the more austere iconography of the new American masters. Only it was an imagery which had been bled out of American painting, just as thoroughly as the more intimate portraiture of the artist's family, which gave a painter like Rivers a way of thinking about his own past through his work.

By the fifties American painting had embarked on what Clement Greenberg called, approvingly in the *Partisan Review*, "a search for the absolute." What mattered was the "pure preoccupation with the invention and arrangement of spaces, surfaces, shapes, colors." "Content," Greenberg continued in a pivotal 1946 essay, "is to be dissolved so completely into form that the work of art cannot be reduced in whole or in part to anything not itself."

And so the lines were drawn. It was Rivers's genius to draw them into a single focus, and with the deftness of an innovator, not an imitator (not even of himself), to recognize his original vision for what it was and then to separate it from the usage to which it had been put. Fine draftsmanship, for example, was not to be an end in itself, a proof of craft, but a tool for unlocking the secret of what fascinated him about a subject—the strangeness in the familiar face of his mother, Sonia Rivers, or friend John Ashbery. In painting, patches of color disconnected from the boundaries of figure pushed the age-old tension between content and form to a new pitch, more stimulating to the eye and brain than the absence of content in the purely visceral arrangement of the superpalette.

By the late fifties and early sixties, through repeated trial, many errors, Rivers had tested the norms of old and new masters alike, and then bent them to his own purposes. Seizing the slashing line and impulsive brushwork of the expressionists, he went on to wield them like magic wands over the moribund images of George Washington Crossing the Delaware, Paul Revere and the Boston Massacre, and the last (and next-to-last) Civil War Veteran. When lat-

er he was to pay homage to the fine art of a Tareyton, a Dutch Master, a Camel, Rivers helped open up the art world to the brand name. But it was when the pressures of the market were clearly outweighed by his interest in the subject at hand that Rivers achieved the greatest emotional impact. In the impromptu sketch of a visitor and, oddly enough, in many of the illustrations and collaborations of the period, Rivers displayed that lively ambiguousness of line and shading that is perhaps his signature. This is the work that grows out of what he has called "an abundance of dissatisfactions": the shiva-limbed portraits that refuse to yield to the eraser, and the paintings which contain the faint remains of all the artist did not want as well as what he did.

Any exceptional work of art is the result of a prolonged and successful struggle, and in the work of these years the elements of Rivers's struggle remained visible. What you see in the finished product is not so different from what you hear in the man talking: a nonstop sifting and sorting of possibilities, sometimes meandering, sometimes capricious, but always intended to move you a bit farther down the road from the known to the unknown.

It is in the late sixties that the mood changes. For Rivers this was a time of loss and change. In 1966, with the accidental death of Frank O'Hara, Rivers lost a friend and collaborator who was as important to his intellectual and social life as his mother-in-law, Berdie, who died nine years earlier, was to his domestic life. In 1968, after a seven-year marriage that produced two daughters, and spanned a period of intense productivity, Rivers was separated from his second wife Clarice. In works like *Don't Fall and 'Me', In Memory of the Dead,* and *The Elimination of Nostalgia,* he commemorated these events. Rivers says he was doing what anthropolo-

gists call "exorcising the spirits." Given the shame that was attached to nostalgia in the fifties and sixties, it took a certain courage, but Rivers was determined to present "these things of the past" in a harsher light.

By the end of the decade multimedia had entered the picture, giving a harder edge to all his work. People like John Ashbery and Norman Mailer appeared punched out of foil, or like artists Jim Dine and Jean Tinguely, cut and pasted and mounted in storm windows, visual happenings on a picture hook. Later, airbrush gave a cleaner look to his work; gone was the history of how a work developed, the starts and stops, the smudges, the fingerprints. But a funny thing happens on the way to success, and by the sixties Rivers was a name to be reckoned with. You meet yourself coming back down the road, and your style has somehow become your trademark.

The distinctive improvisational quality of Rivers's work appeared to him now as the " 'Larry Rivers's' product." He began to feel that he was imitating himself—"I mean, how many times can you just smudge and erase? Who are you kidding?" Or was it that pressure of the market to produce something new? In any event, after *The History of the Russian Revolution,* a monumental assemblage completed in 1966, Rivers stopped drawing freehand and turned to projection. Drawn by an ancient longing in man to have some objective way of reproducing things, he began to project the finished images, photographs and tracings that were to constitute a picture, and then to flesh them out. Speaking of the grandstand portraits of John Ashbery and Rembrandt's *Polish Rider* executed in 1978, Rivers explains, "It's like a child's filling in. . . . You're filling, filling, filling, then finally it gets to the edge—it's there! Then you begin to do the things you do in the other kind of work. It gives me less anxiety. Before there were so many changes."

In the art world, what the painter Jack Tworkov once described as "commercial fine art" was fast overtaking the bold experimentalism of the forties and fifties. "The commercial fine artist," according to Tworkov, was one who worked "directly for the market, making an object of high fashion that will look like pioneering art, only it will look more sleek." [1] Abstract art had proved to be just as susceptible to stylization as mass art; the audience was more affluent but not necessarily more discriminating. Standard brands in "action" painting, color-keyed to executive suites became as common as Campbell soup cans. Twenty years after the publication of "Avant-garde and Kitsch," Clement Greenberg's indictment of the latter might have applied equally to the former: "Another mass product of Western industrialism, it has gone on a triumphal tour of the world . . . so that it is now by way of becoming a universal culture." As Rivers and O'Hara quipped as early as 1961: "They say action is painting. Well, it isn't, and we all know abstract expressionism and pop art have moved to the suburbs." [2]

It was in this period that Larry

Rivers, who had already established himself in London, Paris, and Venice as a kind of madcap Jewish cowboy of the New York School, moved into the lecture and talk-show circuits in a big way. This was the time when the demand for fast-food nourishment in the realm of culture (as in politics) was at its peak. Artist-personalities were catapulted into electronic orbit to propound ideas on just about everything but what they actually did—a phenomenon which has surely contributed to the devaluation of the ideas of the period, as well as to a current uncertainty about its achievements. Rivers himself—whose survival quotient runs high precisely because he never stops working—suggests now that it was then that he began to lose a certain confidence in what he was doing. "What was I about? What about me was filtered by the very way that I presented myself?" he wonders. "After all, everybody makes up their own myth, their own story."

The power of the myth, like the career demands that plague the successful artist, had begun to compete with those internal sources of creativity without which there can be no development. By the seventies, ever more lucrative commissions took a certain toll as well.

Put these pressures in the cooker of the seventies, when the cultural and intellectual ferment of the postwar era had all but dried up (and America as a world power was in sharp decline), and you have the ingredients for that withering away of personal inspiration and public support which Rivers laments in *Drawings and Digressions.* In the end, it is this most worldly of men, who really believes that "it is life we are interested in, not art," who finds himself alone. "Is this what finally happens?" Rivers asks. "You separate yourself from everything that's going on and you just do what you do, what you like? . . . Where am I going to be replenished from? Myself constantly? I'm boring. . . . It's hard to think that it could all come from yourself."

Larry Rivers is too much of a social animal to stay in this corner for long, and it is finally his vision of art as a vehicle for bringing the world into sharper personal focus that carries him beyond despair and the burnout of his generation. "I paint," he says, "and then I can talk about my work in a way that deals with the world." Conversely, Rivers's work offers the curious a way back into the world he paints.

Either way *Drawings and Digressions* takes a giant step toward closing the gap that survives in American culture between an appreciation of art and an understanding of the human conditions which nourish and give it form.

[1] Dorothy Gees Sickler, "Artist in America: Victim of the Culture Boom," *Art in America* (December 1963).

[2] Larry Rivers and Frank O'Hara, "How to Proceed in the Arts," *Evergreen Review,* July-August 1961).

CHRONOLOGY

1923	Born August 17, Bronx, New York	1944	Studied at Juilliard School of Music, New York	1947	Attended Hans Hofmann's school in New York and Provincetown
1940	Began musical career as jazz saxophonist		Member of jazz bands around New York	1948	Began studies at New York University, New York
1942	Enlisted in the U.S. Army Air Corps	1945	Began painting	1949	Exhibition: Jane Street Gallery, New York
1943	Received medical discharge from the armed forces	1946	Married Augusta Burger. Son Joseph born	1950	Traveled in Europe
			Separated from Augusta		

As baby, 1924

1948

As jazz musician, 1945

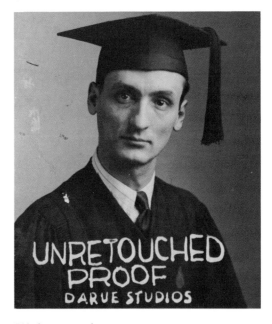

With cap and gown, 1953

15

With Berdie, Water Mill, 1953

With plaster sculpture, 1954

With Maxine Groffsky, 1957. *Photo: John Gruen*

With Marisol, 1957. *Photo: John Gruen*

1951	Received B.A. from New York University in Art Education	1954	Exhibition of sculpture: Stable Gallery, New York	1961	Exhibition: Dwan Gallery, Los Angeles
	Exhibition: Tibor deNagy Art Gallery, mounted by representative John Meyers. Showed at Tibor deNagy every year (except 1955) until his departure from the gallery in 1963. Began making plaster sculpture	1955	Awarded third prize, the 24th Biennial Exhibition of Contemporary Oil Paintings, Corcoran Gallery of Art, Washington,D.C., for *Self-Figure*		Married Clarice Price
				1961–62	Nine months visit to Paris
				1962	Exhibition: Gimpel Fils, London
		1957	Death of mother-in-law, Berdie Burger	1963	Exhibition: Dwan Gallery, Los Angeles
1953	Completed *Washington Crossing the Delaware,* first work acquired by major museum (Museum of Modern Art)		Began working in welded metal sculpture	1964	Traveled in Europe
					Daughter Gwynne born
		1960	Exhibition of sculpture: Martha Jackson Gallery		Exhibition: Gimpel Fils, London

1965	Retrospective exhibition of 170 paintings, drawings, sculpture, and prints: Rose Art Museum, Brandeis University; toured Pasadena Art Museum; The Jewish Museum, New York; Detroit Institute of Arts, Minneapolis Institute of Arts	1966	Death of close friend Frank O'Hara Daughter Emma born	1970	Began work with videotape Exhibition of drawings: Art Institute of Chicago
		1967	Separated from Clarice Price Trip to Africa to make TV film with Pierre Gaisseau	1970–71	Exhibition: Marlborough Gallery, New York
		1968	Trip to Africa to complete film	1973	Exhibition: Marlborough Gallery, New York

Water Mill, Long Island, 1961. *Back row, left to right:* Lisa de Kooning; Frank Perry; Eleanor Perry; John Myers; Anne Porter; Fairfield Porter; Angelo Torricini; Arthur Gold; Jane Wilson; Kenward Elmslie; Paul Brach; Jerry Porter; Nancy Ward; Katharine Porter. *Second row, left to right:* Joe Hazan, Clarice Rivers, Kenneth Koch, Larry Rivers. *Seated on couch:* Miriam Shapiro (Brach), Robert Fizdale, Jane Freilicher, Joan Ward, John Kacere, Sylvia Maizell. *Kneeling on the right, back to front:* Alvin Novak, Bill de Kooning, Jim Tommaney. *Front row:* Stephen Rivers, William Berkson, Frank O'Hara, Herbert Machiz. *Photo: John Gruen*

With Clarice and baby Gwynne, 1965. *Photo Kathryn Abbe*

At work, 1967

17

Patsy Southgate, Bill Berkson, John Ashbery, (*front*) Frank O'Hara, Kenneth Koch, 1965

With Bob Rauschenberg (*left*) and Henry Geldzahler, 1969

In N. Africa, 1964

At work, 1977

DRAWINGS AND DIGRESSIONS
BY
LARRY RIVERS

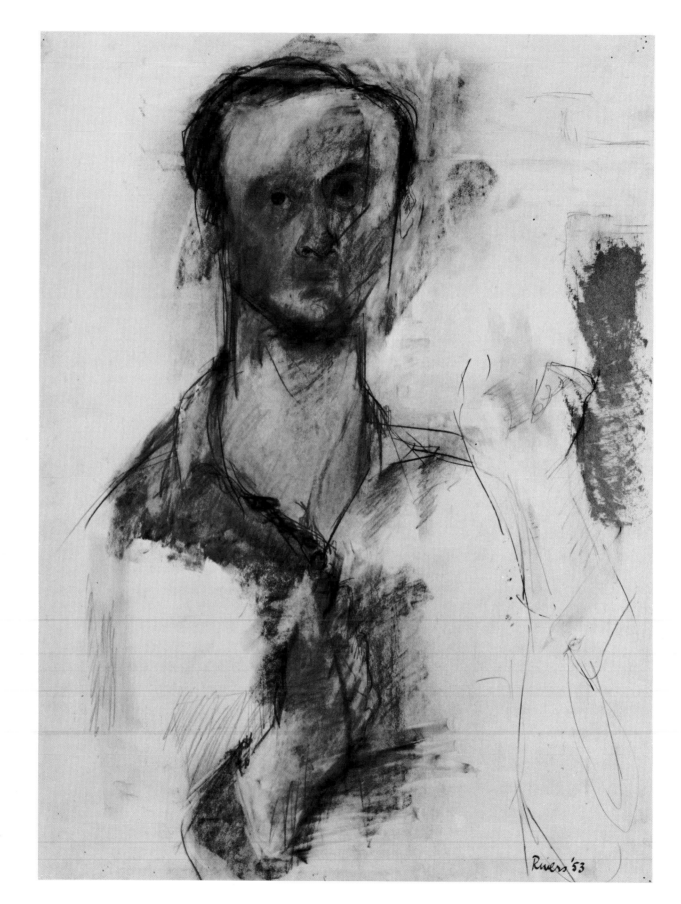

Self-Portrait, 1953

BEGINNINGS: EARLY LIFE AND WORK

I think Oscar Wilde once said it: life follows art. There's this whole big world out in front of you, you see things . . . trees, dogs, streets . . . but it's only when someone comes along and gives them a certain focus that you see that *particular* thing. Well I had a romance about the Impressionists. I mean, that's what brought me into art. I perceived their work and loved it; it's very soft; by now it seems sentimental, pretty, like so many French movies. But even as late as the fifties when the world didn't look like that anymore, I was able to find corners that had Impressionist overtones. If I looked out a window in the Bronx where I grew up, where there were billboards and loud noises and gasoline odors, I could see the roofs and the trees mixed in a certain old nineteenth-century way. The Impressionists—they were my heroes.

I began to really see myself as an artist in the late forties, sort of early. At Hans Hofmann's art school that concentrated on abstract art I began to have a fantastic desire to draw realistically. It's strange—in relation to the march of events—my interests were really perennial interests. I wanted to be an artist in

the classic sense: "Methinks I have to draw." It sounds corny today, but that's what it was like for me. By the time the forties and fifties came around, that was not the idea anymore. To be an artist was *something else*, some combination of being an interesting person, a forward-looking person, knowledgeable about history, especially art history, someone who wouldn't accept the usual standards of things. You set yourself up as some kind of special agent for handling these supposedly different things. If your mother liked the sunset it wasn't the proper subject matter for a painting.

But somewhere sneaking underneath all this was the idea that I wanted to identify with the *history* of art. I wanted to have some of the abilities of the best to really prove to myself that there was something of the artist in me.

In the beginning, I didn't really understand the modern French masters at all. Picasso was interesting because he seemed to represent something modern. Whatever it was, it looked like it must be good because everybody said it was good and it was so *peculiar.* But I didn't get it really. I started with Bonnard. I just began drawing the figure. I would ride with a pad on the bus. Everywhere I went I made quick sketches.

But as the fifties wore on it dawned on me that I had to find something personal. I was very interested in nudes—it was the awakening of sex in myself. I had done a paradise painting in 1948, all nudes, Bonnard nudes, about ten! These women were draped in casement windows—I was so far out of this world, I was dreaming up castles. Ingres's *Women in a Turkish Bath* may have had some influence on me, but I did it in a Bonnard style. Then I covered that painting with a painting of Christ kneeling in the garden, the moment before he was crucified. It was insane.

What would life have been like if I hadn't become an artist? I don't know. I'm fairly politically minded; I'm interested in history and people. I don't know what I would have done with it. Maybe having been taken seriously as an artist enabled me to take myself seriously in reading history and in thinking about politics. I think you have to succeed in some world to even believe that any of your interests are valid. If I didn't have some kind of assurance from art, I don't know what I would have done.

But I don't know these days. I don't mean I'm going through Herculean doubts right now, but I do wonder . . . I don't really care about what's going on in the art world to a great degree—except insofar as it touches me. When you are younger you're interested in seeing where you are, how you're doing, and things like that.

And when you're older, and in my case fairly established, you don't run around anymore feeling as if you *have* to see this show, that show. It is possible that a lot of drive comes from wanting to establish yourself, and that once you've done that, some drive is gone. And maybe that brings you back to basics. But I think it really goes the other way.

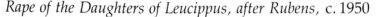

Rape of the Daughters of Leucippus, after Rubens, c. 1950

A Street in the Bronx, 1951

I wonder if my interest in art was always just an interest in myself. What I mean is do I go out and look? Do I look at the turn of a Cezanne apple? Do I go see a Caravaggio darkness? I produce art, I make art. Is it out of some overall interest in art, or is it just a constant concern with myself as an artist, having been identified as an artist, and continuing that identity?

Maybe I'm not being very original with that ques-tion. Maybe it's always been a duality: the artist is interested in himself and in art. After all, when you start to work you are almost always led by your ego, but at some point you drop that to see what you've found. Like me, you may separate yourself from everything that's going on and you just do what you do, what you like, but you are still part of the art world.

Middle Europe, Double Portrait of Myself, 1954

"It was Tolstoy who made the grand abstraction that a man's life is a reaction to his face. When my face began to be this one, say about fourteen or fifteen, some very fierce stubborn melancholy set in. At most, it was going to be tolerated. Never desired. To have a face that is day-by-day growing to look like a hawk, or an eagle, not to mention the meanest 1930s notion of one of the Elders of Zion, gave me a sense of injustice that must account for the particular combination of doubt and chutzpah that I recognize as me."
—*Art in America*

This is an early self-portrait. Strangely enough, the one on the left would be a fantastic likeness of my father's youngest brother, who was three years older than I. And the one on the right reminds me of myself in a certain kind of Yiddish-European tradition. It's a more sensitive-looking person than that central view, which is harder—there's something wrong with him.

In the single self-portrait, my hand is clutching my shirt. I have something wrong with my left hand and in order to keep the hand steady when I drew myself, the left hand had to be held still so that I could get to look at it. I didn't do many self-portraits. I just didn't like my face and I felt that I would be too prone to want to alter the reality, and so I decided that not only did I not want to face what I looked like, but I didn't want that quality of character which might lie and draw other kinds of features. So I haven't done many.

"I grew up in the streets of what was much less inhabited in those days—the Bronx. The only things in our house resembling art were a cheap tapestry, a cross between a Fragonard and a Minsky popular in many dining rooms in the twenties, and a five-and-ten-cent store 8" by 10" reproduction of a Spanish *señorita* holding a flower just above an exposed breast, a painting which, to make matters worse, followed us from one apartment to another. Mind you, when I took my mother to her first exhibition of paintings—she having had such a profound dining room education in art—she told me which were good paintings and which were bad in a *very* strong voice. But if I've inherited natural bad taste I'd praise my parents for passing on to me their strength, their natural physical endurance and animal concentration. So much in the making of art is energy. Not just the manipulation of the arm or fingers, but the physical insistence of the mind to keep on making decisions—in spite of continuous physical and mental disruption." —*Horizon*

This is a drawing of Pavlova which was quite a technical accomplishment for me in those days. It hung in my mother's bedroom until the day my mother died and my sister put it in *her* bedroom.

Pavlova, "Le Papillon," 1953

The Artist's Mother, 1953

This is my mother. Up until this point I had never made a drawing of her, but by the time '53 rolled around, and I was thirty, she was beginning to realize I was hopeless—I was never going to be anything but this. Before, my mother thought art was a good hobby for me. Like a lot of mothers they worry about how you are going to make a living. I think she was really worried about having to give me money—because if you don't make a living, a good mother can't see you starve, right? The anxiety parents have about children making a living—myself included—is not always an altruistic concern. . . . Anyway, by '53 I had begun to be compensated. Gloria Vanderbilt bought a painting of mine for $750, which at that time sounded like the most fantastic amount of money. The idea that someone had given me $750 changed my mother overnight. "Maybe you got something there." And by the time she posed for this drawing she was already convinced that she was doing something that was either helping me or that she was involved in some activity that had professional status.

From a psychological point of view, my mother has

a rather sad look here. I think that I read that into her and in this particular drawing it came out. I've always thought of my mother as a sourpuss. I never really liked her face. I always held it against her for what I looked like. I had that kind of relationship to my parents and their faces: they were foreigners, they couldn't speak English, they were a constant embarrassment. . . . Actually, I have seen photographs of her when she was younger—she was pretty attractive. My father thought she was good-looking, which I always liked. He'd say, "She gets better all the time." I think she's in her late fifties here. She died in 1975 and she was in her eighties. She did pretty well.

Erasures played a great part in drawings like this. Erasure accounted for grays and the graduation of tones; it created a certain kind of color for me.

This is another drawing of my mother. It catches something else in her. She went from being a very positive kind of monster to a rather questioning, hopeless old lady who didn't know what the hell she was doing on this earth. My father died and she had no one to boss around anymore—but these pictures were drawn at the point where she still had spunk and quite a bit of aggression. She could be a pain in the ass.

Until she was a very old woman, my mother actually used to inspire me to throw things at her. She would come to Southampton and visit, and after the strength that I had mustered for the first few days began to wane—and she'd get picking—I don't know, she didn't mean it probably, but I would start to throw things at her. I wouldn't hit her, but I would, you know, let her know how I felt.

Front Face and Profile of Artist's Mother, 1953

Family Group, 1957

This is an unfinished drawing done from one of those classic photographs taken on the occasion of my grandfather's visit from Russia or Poland. There were twenty-one people posing for this picture, and I just couldn't see my way through doing them all.

I don't know who or what master I had in mind. I think the style here is one of those "naturalisms" that just sort of come down to you. . . . As to why I left it unfinished, you can take three or four points of view. It wasn't *necessary* to finish it; I lost interest in it; or you can just accept it as a certain kind of style. It takes a certain chutzpah to say, "Well, look, I do what I can do and what I can't do I don't care about."

But what really lies at the bottom of this is an interest in my own family and the situation called up by that photograph. As I'm drawing I'm thinking about these people. I'm thinking about how to draw and what their eyes look like and I'm also thinking of them. It's a curious experience which allows me to daydream about a certain time, about what it was like, about having to run up to my grandfather and give him a kiss when I didn't want to because he had a big long beard. So here's another way of thinking about your past, using the convention of art. . . . Right now as I'm thinking about it, I just realized that my grandfather left Europe in 1934, about a year or two after Hitler actually came to power, and yet he obviously didn't dream that it had any meaning for him because he went back and, of course, perished. Every time I look at this I think about the subject and something comes up. The age of different people, how many are dead, all those kinds of things.

This is *the* family at the bar mitzvah celebration. The man is my mother's brother and this is a woman he was married to who committed suicide about five or six years later. She called her son, my cousin, up to the roof—she wasn't satisfied to just do it. She called him up to the roof and then did it in front of him. Quite upset. I think she thought her husband was having an affair with another woman. Probably true—but why get *that* serious about it?

What year was it? '61. I'm beginning to get deeper into subject matter that really interests me, but I don't have the apparatus to portray it realistically. That's my uncle, the guy who has a moustache. I was always amused by this—a Jew trying to look like Adolf Hitler. I arrived at some conventions to get features in a quick

way without laboring for a certain kind of realism— like two black charcoal dots for the nose—and I'm even getting touches of a kind of child in the white of the girl's dress, a kind of little Shirley Temple. There's even a touch of the evening-gown look there, though it was just done with brushes which were maybe four or five inches wide. By this point I'm thinking that I'm Franz Kline. Look what I made out of a pair of pants; I'm making these very big broad shapes.

I'd love to see that photograph again and do another one. I feel I want to devote a whole year to them. At any rate, at this point I'm overexpressing my ethnic background with these things from photographs. Ten, fifteen years earlier, maybe even more, I changed my name from Grossberg to Rivers. So that lies with me in

Bar Mitzvah Photograph Painting, 1961

my subconscious somewhere. Later on I am able to ravage the whole subject in another way because while I would be bothered by the Jewish last name traveling as a jazz musician in the South, and very happy that I had a very neutral name like Rivers, somewhere it must have bothered me. My family always used to say, "Well, why do you have to change—are you ashamed of Grossberg?" And I never would admit that. But in all probability it was whatever Jews go through with those things—names and noses, and I had 'em all. I had all the bugs, all the neuroses. So later on I'm wondering if it's some way of proving that I'm not ashamed of it at all. I'm not. I'm very interested in the subject and prove it by devoting quite a few paintings to these scenes.

The "Rejected" stamp doesn't have the psychological undertones you might think. It is a convention that had to do with the old photography studios. They'd send you ten photos and the families would be able to make a choice. Knowing the working-class ethics in those days, the photographic studios put something on that photo which wouldn't allow you to just keep it. They'd have something like "La Russe Studios" or "Rejected Copy" somewhere very large on the photograph so you couldn't copy it. And I was using letters at that time—I was very interested in stenciling.

Family photograph: artist with his mother, father, and sisters, 1938

Wedding Photo Drawing—1938, 1961

Now this is a drawing that I did of a photo taken in 1938, and it's a wedding of a cousin of mine where the convention was for each family to line up and pose for the photographer en masse. Actually, I'm completely unrecognizable in the original photograph.

Somewhere along the line, around '60, '61, I began doing a whole series called *Me.* And in some way this drawing is like an early sputtering of that idea. *Me* contained photos from my childhood that my parents and uncles had saved, picnics, bar mitzvahs, things like that. I think I felt some kind of historical substantiation when Arshile Gorky did one of himself and *his* mother. But I just wanted to do it. Back as far as '56 I did a painting called *Europe,* which is based on a photograph taken in the twenties in Poland of a cousin and his family. And so this is just another one of those. I think that by the time '61 came around, and I did this you see a loss of interest or a shame in a certain kind of realistic detail. I'm passing myself off as some kind of artist interested in a kind of scribble, in certain kinds of arrangements of form. But I was also interested in the subject. As a matter of fact, what has finally happened is that I'm doing a whole other version now almost twenty years later. I mean, it's a long life, right?

My parents couldn't stand their names. Everyone called my mother something different. As a Jew she was called Sura. Her Russian name was Sonya, and when she came here she was Shirley. My father's name was Shiah. They called him Sam.

Papa a Little Later, 1964

Within the image: For Mama 1964 / Larry Rivers

Mama a Little Later, 1964

Portrait of Jane Freilicher, 1950

Jane Freilicher was responsible for my really becoming an artist. . . . It was 1945; I was playing in a band and her husband at that time was a guy called Jack Freilicher who was a pianist. Jack and I were in the same band traveling up the East Coast, and during the afternoons while the guys played poker, she, her husband and I kind of did "art." And she began to praise what I did. We went for long walks and I don't know, I never met a girl like her. She was very serious, like a guy in the sense that you could have a conversation with her—I'm talking about being twenty-one years old. And she suggested that I go to Hans Hofmann's art school. Then she joined me.

We were hung up on looking at the Impressionists and the post-Impressionists. I began to separate from that pretty quickly but she held on. She does still life and looks out a window at a landscape; she wants to struggle with that. At the same time she's very intelligent, *funny* girl, but she doesn't seem to think that that can translate itself into a change of subject matter. But why should she?

I think that all along she just felt that she didn't get what she wanted. I don't know what there was to "get," but she's that way and it's marvelous that she is. I'm more sympathetic to it now. For a while I kind of turned her rejection of me into my rejection of her work. But I see that she's kept to it. She's got something. She just sticks to her flowers and her oranges and her fruit, and looking out the window—its her art arena—and she has gotten very good at it. But you

"Aside from his theories of art, like 'push and pull,' Hans Hofmann made art glamorous by including in the same sentence with the names Michelangelo, Rubens, Courbet, and Matisse, the name *Rivers*—and his own, of course. It wasn't that you were a Michelangelo or a Matisse, but that you faced somewhat similar problems. What he really did by talking this way was to inspire you to work. He had his finger on the most important thing in an artist's life, which is the conviction that art has an existence and a glamorous one at that. He puts you on the path with the desire to go somewhere. What you find along the way is your own

never get any idea from her art that she really has quite a nutty mind.

problem. *My* problem back then in 1947 was that when I started drawing in the presence of a nude female model, all that found its way onto my pages were three peculiar rectangles. At the end of a year I became frantic to draw the figure, and in a way that is no more advanced than Corot. If I didn't do this, I'd never be able to convince myself of my genius. To want to draw like Corot, or, for that matter, any master, was more related to *identification* than to the creation of an original work. It was important to me to solidify my position, to be able to say, 'Yes, don't worry, you are really an artist.' " —*Horizon*

After Rembrandt, c.1951

Strangely enough, when I went to Paris in 1950 I was thinking to myself "maybe I'm not an artist." I sat around Paris and I wrote poetry the entire time I was there. I saw Paris and thought how beautiful-sad life is and how beautiful-sad these poems are and I didn't really do much painting. I did really more living. I was twenty-six and I was just wondering what life was about and I was trying to see what art was about. I went to museums and I saw marvelous works in the Louvre. I went to a few shows. When I went to Paris I wanted to see the home of the Impressionists, the Cubists, the home of painting really.

I think I suffered a few emotional setbacks in Paris. I met a girl or two that nothing worked out with as usual. So I stayed alone a lot in this apartment and wrote. I'd go out at night—I probably was acting out some nineteenth-century idea of the artist searching for experience. Paris seems to have represented that kind of place—it may still represent that for some people. It's a kind of sensitive city, a place where sensitive men gather; it's a little stupid, but these atmospheres prevail in all sorts of ways. You can think it's stupid on Monday and on Tuesday have another sense of what it's all about.

Robertus, after Holbein, 1954

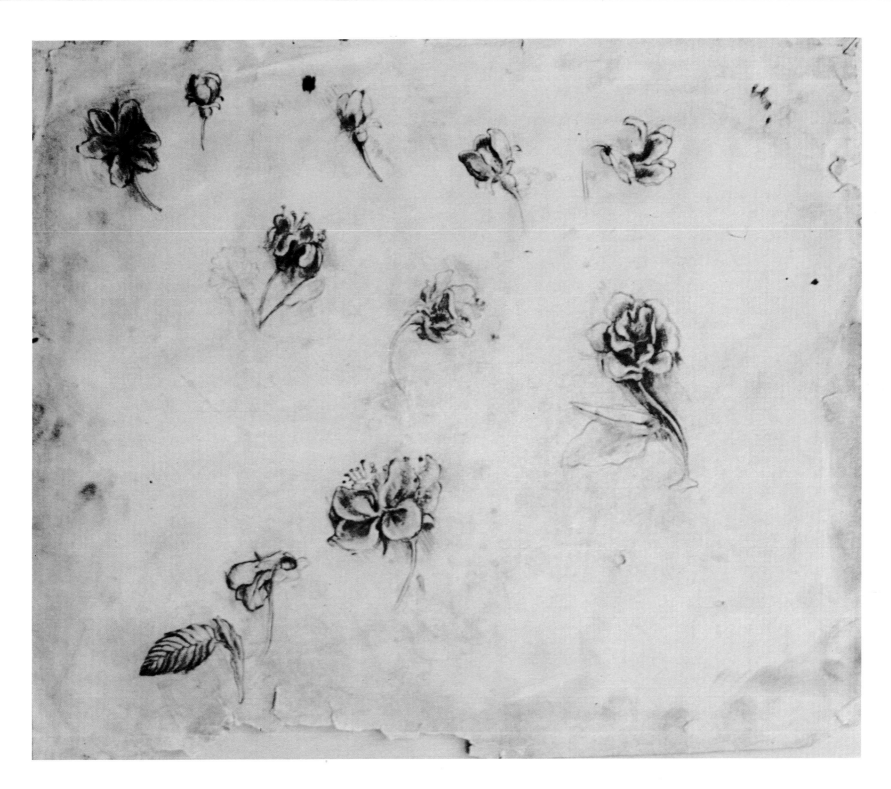

Flower Studies, after Leonardo, 1954

This is my da Vinci period. I think there is a page of his work just like this—it's straight from da Vinci. No tracing, no nothing, this is completely free. In those days I probably would have thought it cheating to trace. And now I project images and trace. I'm the biggest cheat, you know, but I don't think of it that way. I feel I've "paid my dues."

Bathers, 1952

This is early '51 when the world discovered that Jackson Pollock was really painting with a stick, and so I started to draw with a stick, dipping it into cans of enamel. This is the result. I had quite a few of them. I think I destroyed most of them. I can never do a drawing which satisfies me that I don't go over. I can't make anything with just a line. Other people can. Claes Oldenburg, for instance: it looks corny, illustrative, yet he gets something—he just goes with his hand.

A Girl with Sad Eyes, 1951

After David, c. 1959

Study for Sculpture, 1951

Castelli's Piece, 1951

This is a sketch for one of my early cement and plaster sculptures. I made it outdoors. Leo Castelli commissioned it, and we had a big party. It sat in his driveway in East Hampton for years. Then one night Jackson Pollock tried to run it down because it was realistic. Philip Guston talked him out of it. But anyway— snow, ice, something happened to it. It's gone.

Head of Woman with Blue Eye, 1952

This is my de Kooning period. 1952. Everyone had it. . .the large eyes from those women-things of his. I hope it has a little bit of otherness in it, I'm not sure.

But I see I started something here. No hair. Like hair wasn't a shape—it was a texture. And so I would cut off heads at foreheads, or where the hairline began.

Two Women, 1952

This is a drawing of Augusta Berger Rivers, a girl I married, the mother of Steven and my son Joseph, and the daughter of Berdie, my mother-in-law—who lived with me for many years and appears in many paintings, one in every museum of New York. I lived with Augusta for a year. She may have been visiting me in Southampton after I was already living with her mother when this picture was drawn. I had the children, so she came out there to visit.

I drew everybody who came to see me. I had this idea that if you weren't drawing, working, painting, sculpting, doing some reading, something about art, you were wasting your time. All my twenties and thirties were lived in that kind of spirit. I mean I was

Reclining Nude (Augusta Burger), c.1953

Augusta, 1953

doing it all the time. I was a burden to a lot of people. I'm not your silent type and when I was drawing someone, I would talk about all sorts of subjects that had nothing to do with the drawing—but of course the people couldn't move. They could talk as much as they wanted except when I came to the mouth.

Once I began there was something so simple about getting the look of someone, doing it direct in pencil. There was no coloration, no orchestration, no question about "What else is there going to be in the work? Where should I place it on the page?" My drawings were like moments.

Augusta in a Rubens World, 1954

For me a three-quarters view like this one is rare. Most of my faces are head-on. I don't know why I did it like this—it even has both eyes, but for some reason it has a certain exuberance that I usually don't get, certain psychological implications which remind me of Rubens. The paper is full of gook and goo and oil and dust gathered in the cellar, but yet there's some sort of old master look about it. . . . In those days people were slightly ashamed of realism—I mean the hipper artists. And so it's really strange that I did this back then.

I still have a relationship with this woman. She's married again and has two children and one of her children came to work for me as an assistant. Augusta called me the other day to say she needed money to go to the dentist. Would I pay? I'm paying. We're in touch.

Years ago we only lived together for a short time. . . . She was a germ freak. I mean she followed germs. As she saw it, a lot of people handle money—people have germs on their hands and they get on the money and then into the cash register. Somebody picks it up and *their* germs get on the money when they give you change. So when Augusta handled money it was as if she were handling disease. When she talked into a phone, she held that phone further away than most people because of the germs that were coming through the line. You couldn't bend over a pot when she cooked food because the germs would fall off your face. I had to take a bath before I could fuck her. I guess it kept me clean for a few years. She's better now, but she used to sit in a chair and stare and I just thought that it would be throwing the children to the wolves to leave them with her. So her mother came to live with me and we raised the boys together.

Two Views of Augusta, 1955

Head of Joseph Rivers, 1957

Joseph Standing, 1954

Joseph Seated, 1954

Steven 14, 1959

Berdie Seated in a Chair, 1953

And here we have Berdie, my mother-in-law, sitting in the garden in Southampton. She was a devoted creature. Berdie is the closest thing I've ever known to a saint. I don't mean that because I'm involved with saints. She had all the signs of even being a little dense, but like saints are thought to be, she had no ego. She seemed to just be glad to be around and happy to be alive.

Her husband had died and she had not very much to do and she didn't have any relatives and she just was glad to sort of be with me and the boys—and took care of them. She was very inept, she could hardly cook. She was nobody's idea of an old-fashioned mother-in-law in that sense. She tried, but she was just bad at it. But at the same time she was very easy to be with. She had very few complaints—it was like, from my point of view, perfect. And she even contributed financially. Her husband left her a very small amount of money, but we did get about $75 a month and I got money from a small disability pension that started from a hand tremor I developed in the Air Corps in 1942, so together we were able to free me to paint without working. And she was very glad to do it and loved my friends and, you know, nothing threw her. I mean,

here she was from a very ordinary Jewish background, born in Harlem when Harlem was still Jews. And there were gay guys in my life and black people and dope addicts and she would say, "Oh, isn't he nice . . . and . . . he's nice . . . and . . . Tennessee Williams is nice." She was slightly mad. A kind of glutton for punishment. The boys would walk all over her, and she'd just come back like the ocean. She was amazing.

This is a work that grew out of a series, and the painting is in the Rhode Island School of Design. This is a very sketchy version, my mother-in-law sitting in the garden in Southampton on one of our innumerable afternoons when I just tried to get another drawing.

I think that in 1953—if not to this very day—I thought, "I can't draw, I better keep trying to draw to see if I can get it." There was something also about the chair she was sitting in—it was very elaborate cane—and I did a whole drawing based on that. And she just posed. I think at that point she hadn't gotten the nerve to take her clothes off. Not that I wanted her to take them off, but finally after a few years she was able to actually get undressed. Didn't care. I said, "What the heck are you embarrassed about?" So she did it. Yet it was against everything in her background.

Berdie's Hand and Feet, 1953

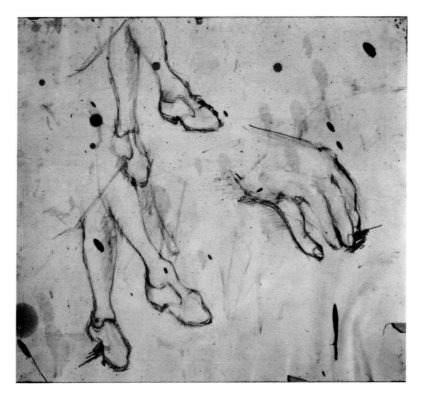

Berdie Pastel, 1953

Half of Berdie Seated, c. 1952

Now I must confess that I don't like this drawing, although from time to time people have said this is the closest I've ever gotten to a thing called the "quick-sketch artist." They seem sort of jovial and kind of quick and I didn't take them too seriously. But at any rate these are Berdie and I think it's the beginning of her posing for me in the nude. You can see why a big fat older woman is good subject matter—she goes in and out and she already makes your drawing for you.

Museums started buying my work at the point that I was painting Berdie and then, you know how they are, they get one painting and then they stop. So it's funny—she's in the Met, in the Modern, and she's in the Brooklyn Museum and she's in the Whitney. That's my mother-in-law. . . . She died in '57. Now twenty-one years. I still remember her well. . . . I'll be there, Berdie.

Quick Sketch of Berdie Nude I, 1955

Quick Sketch of Berdie Nude II, 1955

Berdie Seated on Bed, study for painting, 1954

This drawing was done for a painting called *The Double Nude of Berdie,* where she's seated on the bed, but it came out quite differently. By the time I started to paint it, her position had shifted and I didn't use the drawing.

Why did I do so many pictures of her? She was available—free. It wasn't that I felt like I was honoring her in some way. I'm very single-minded and selfish. She was just available and quiet. And I could do anything I wanted. I mean, since she had such an underdeveloped ego, I could never insult her by my work. With other people, if you draw them or take a portrait commission, there's always that aspect of, "Oh, is that what I look like?" or they're nervous about whether I'm getting their essential handsomeness or femaleness or something. Berdie had none of that. She looked at it, she sort of laughed at some. I didn't have any explaining to do. I would just say "sit" and I'd start to work, whereas with everybody else—even people as friendly and as knowledgeable as Frank O'Hara—there was some kind of conversation that had to go on because everybody feels some social compunction to be interesting or entertaining.

This is '54. I had already done *Washington Crossing the Delaware* and I had gone through a whole period of that kind of painting—wiping, painting, wiping, charcoal—and then suddenly I had a day when I went *Bop*! I didn't want it anymore. And I started to move in another direction. By the time I was doing this work I was really getting every little light that fell on the body and I was getting certain details that I had never before investigated. I started to try and work with very small brushes less than a half inch wide.

Claes Oldenburg once said that I seemed to continue beyond anybody's point of belief. I mean I kept *at* something so long that it maybe finally becomes something. I don't know if it was a compliment or an insult—he was acting as if he really couldn't stand what I do, but you know, if I flatter myself into thinking that maybe I've done something, I just do keep at it. But I never think of myself as a person with patience at all; it's just that I want to get things so badly that I keep at it. I always think that I'd like to get something the first second I do it. The first second—I just want to get it all. And I don't. And then it becomes a matter of not being able to stand that anybody would see it bad. And so I'm undoing it, undoing it, correcting it, just to try to get it. It isn't out of some idea of perfection.

This last one depresses me because I don't own it. It's called *Southampton Backyard*. My mother-in-law was still alive and she's in the garden here. There's a car or motorcycle. It was at that certain point when I was still adhering to a certain kind of realism and not worrying about it, and yet beginning to break away from it as you can see with these shapes and wipings and things like that. But there's enough in there that you can really feel the landscape quite strongly.

I had moved out to the country by then—I was like those people who think of solving problems by geographical change; I was in some turmoil and thought I'd go to the country and really paint. And in certain ways it was also like imitating my old model: the

Southampton Backyard, 1956

Watermill Landscape, 1953

Impressionists. You wake up, it's kind of quiet; you go out there and you do your drawing and your painting; you're out there with the green grass and hoping, you know, for the best. I haven't seen this photograph or this work since I did it. I'm thrilled to see it.

Here is one of the last attempts I made at trying to do something about landscape. I had to find a scene where there was a barn or a tree, or maybe a cow. I didn't know what to do with flat fields, rows of trees twenty miles away. I can't stand things where you can't see details.

I don't mind this one, it's OK, but I began to realize that my days with landscapes were drawing to a close. When I think of what the hell the Impressionists did—and Corot! Corot! How he could paint trees and silvery little leaves. Extraordinary. So I just realized, well, OK, they did it and no one is going to come close to them—forget it.

Washington Crossing the Delaware, 1953

WASHINGTON CROSSING THE DELAWARE

1953. I was living in Southampton. I had just read Tolstoy's *War and Peace*, a work of art based on an actual event in the history of Russia. I wanted to make a work of art that included some aspect of national life, and so I chose Washington Crossing the Delaware. It was like getting into the ring with Tolstoy.

The only thing was that Washington Crossing the Delaware was always like the dopiest, funniest thing in American life. Year after year, as a kid in school, you see these amateurish plays that are completely absurd but you know they represent patriotism—love of country, so here I am choosing something that everybody has this funny duality about. It was also a way for me to just stick out my thumb at other people. I suddenly carved out a little corner for myself. It seems to be something in my nature—I seem to fall on things that have a double edge. . . . Today there doesn't seem to be anything to oppose. I mean, everything is as tentative as everything else—realism, abstraction. . . .

Luckily for me I didn't give a crap about what was going on at the time in New York painting. In fact, I was energetic and egomaniacal and, what is even more important, cocky and angry enough to want to do something no one in the New York art world could doubt was *disgusting, dead*, and *absurd*. So what could be dopier than a painting dedicated to a national cliché—Washington Crossing the Delaware. The last painting that dealt with George and the rebels is hanging in the Met and was painted by a coarse German nineteenth-century academician named Leutze who really loved Napoleon more than anyone and thought crossing a river on a late December afternoon was just another excuse for a general to assume a heroic, slightly tragic pose. What could have inspired him I'll never know. What *I* saw in the crossing was quite different. I saw the moment as nerve-racking and uncomfortable. I couldn't picture anyone getting into a chilly river around Christmas time with anything resembling hand-on-chest heroics.

"When I did *Washington Crossing the Delaware*, it took about seven years for people to finally come around to the fact that maybe I did something that was the beginning of something new. Because of Pollock and everybody's preoccupation with a certain kind of abstract art, it just seemed like something that fell down in the middle of nowhere for no reason. It's the same thing that I think is happening now. . . . Maybe my work just seems to fall into the old-fashioned idea of subject matter, and so they don't see yet that it requires anything new from them in talking about it."

—*Arts Magazine*

Emanuel Leutze, *Washington Crossing the Delaware*, 1851

Study for *Washington Crossing the Delaware*, 1953

Study for *Washington Crossing the Delaware,* 1953

Study for *Washington Crossing the Delaware*, 1953

Study for *Washington Crossing the Delaware*, 1953

Study for *Washington Crossing the Delaware*, 1953

Study for *Washington Crossing the Delaware*, 1953

Study for *Washington Crossing the Delaware*, 1953

Study for *Washington Crossing the Delaware*, 1953

Study for *Washington Crossing the Delaware*, 1953

Study for *Washington Crossing the Delaware*, 1953

Study for *Washington Crossing the Delaware*, 1953

Study for *Washington Crossing the Delaware*, 1953

Study for *Washington Crossing the Delaware*, 1953

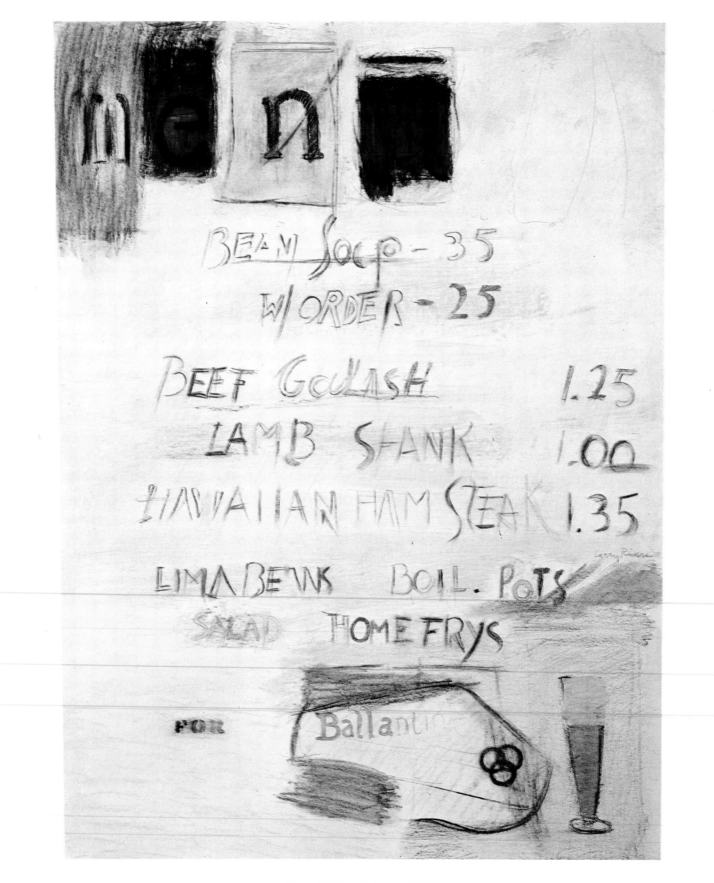

Golden Oldies: Menu, 1978

THREE

CEDAR BAR: FRIENDS AND THE ART WORLD

By the early fifties American painting had suddenly become an international commodity. There was a burgeoning of art activity, art interest; more and more money went into it, and in some way it really was a part of the emergence of America as a world power. After the destruction of Europe, the money was here. And instead of America looking toward Europe, Europe began to look toward America, and we went in to ourselves. Culture no longer had to be found in Europe. And one little microcosm that represented that whole thing was the Cedar Tavern on University Place.

You had painters coming in there and poets—all my friends went there—Kenneth Koch, Frank O'Hara, John Ashbery, Arnold Weinstein, all writers; Howie Kanovitz, a painter. And it was about sex too. What is a bar? Figured it out the other day—all it is, is about sex, really. And loneliness.

When you went to the bar de Kooning was there and Franz Kline and Milton Resnick, and every writer who wrote about art ... everybody would come down. That was the place to go—it was a scene. It was absolutely fantastic in that way. Women came in, parties emanated from there. It had a certain kind of exuberance, and every day and every night you could just drop in before you went home. It was your neighborhood bar, but the neighborhood was really the art community, the downtown art community.

When I was on the $64,000 Question in 1957 and won $32,000 answering questions about "Contemporary Art," I bought drinks on the house. It was like a movie scene, and the check was grabbed from my hand and passed around the entire bar so that everybody could take a look at what I had won. It was really the sort of community that doesn't exist now.

Whether or not the Cedar was a kind of incubator for certain attitudes toward art is another question. I can't really pin down any aesthetic I came away with. It was more like a place to find out what was going on, what was happening. It was a verbal news shop— who's fucking whom, who's going to show whom, who's going to what gallery, who just sold a large work. It was like that—and whatever you want to make of it, you can.

Every so often Jackson Pollock, who was already out in the country, would storm into the bar. He was getting to be very well known and his works were beginning to sell. I think he was going to a psychiatrist. By evening he'd be kind of drunk and stagger in and make a scene. He was like the all-American rough-and-tumble-drunk-type guy; he was a big cornball—the kind of person that I'm not used to. I mean, I knew the children of Europeans; I really didn't know those Americans who come on like—*"Hey Man, how ya doin'?"* He was like that. When he was sober he was very morose; drunk he was all over the place in a sort of sloppy, emotional way. But he had a certain power. You knew it. When he was in a room you felt his presence, very much.

When he came in he would do something outrageous to every person there. I was known in the circle to be someone who took heroin, so he would make signs about pushing a needle into his arm. Or if a guy was gay, he'd talk about sucking cocks or something. He was so simple and clear—he was sort of funny.

Most of the artists in the Cedar Bar were abstract artists. I was the only one who was painting realisti-cally, and I felt very self-conscious about it. I felt as if I should be accepted: I'm an artist and I like big paintings and I appreciated what they were doing; aspects of their work even crept into my realism, but I wanted different things. I wanted to tell a different story. So from that point of view they didn't influence me, but maybe being exposed to what seems to be the opposite of your work is a very good thing. Every day you're listening to other ideas coming out of other kinds of inspiration, so that maybe at the base of my "realism" there was some other thing that made it richer. I don't know. I remember being asked by groups that were painting realistically at that time if I would join them in some kind of political art action. "Look at those guys," they would say about the abstract painters, "look how far they're getting, look at what they're doing to American art—they're getting into all the shows and all the museums and people are collecting them. Here we are;" they said, "why don't we try to band together and fight these guys?" I never joined them. I identified much more with the abstract artists.

Brushes and Cooper's Hawk, 1956

Here's a pastel of John Ashbery who at the time couldn't have been more than in his early thirties. Already he looks like an old baggy poet. He was a member of my inner circle who would go to a party, drink a lot, eat his meal, ask to be excused, leave the table, fall asleep on a bed, and when he woke up he'd say good night to everybody and go out to the bars and start drinking all over again.

He was easy to draw, but he didn't have the same relationship to my drawings that Frank O'Hara had. When O'Hara posed for you it was about the drawing—it was about you and your art. John more or less countenanced the experience. He would allow himself to be drawn; he was not interested in the results. He was and is smart about art. He's remained my friend. In fact, I just did a painting of him. Now he's a Pulitzer Prize-winner and I make a grandstand portrait of him, right? It's him typing, and his poem "Pyrography" runs, across the top half of the painting.

In the early sixties I told an interviewer from *Art in America* that one could go into art as a career the same as law, medicine, or government. "Only the poets remain pure," I said. There wasn't any money attached to poetry then, and at that time no one made such a fuss over the poets who were my friends, and so they were forced to remain pure—there was no other way for poets to be. But times have changed.

Still there is a certain purity to a poem. You can take a painting off the wall the way you can buy a pair of shoes. You can pick it out, they wrap it up, it's yours—you take it home. You hang it up on your wall. It's like putting a pair of shoes on your feet—"These are *my* shoes." You don't own a John Ashbery poem. But you can own a Larry Rivers painting. And so it's a commodity in a way poetry never really is.

But at the same time, the poet himself can become a commodity in the same way that an artist can. John Ashbery goes on 55,000 lectures and Kenneth Koch is now writing books on how to teach poetry to Italian children. I mean what has that got to do with "poetry"?

A woman came over to me the other day and said, "You had a *wonderful* drawing of John Ashbery at the Museum." I thought it was the new painting she was talking about, but it was a 1953 drawing I did of John Ashbery. She says, "You know, I have to be honest with you. You know why I liked it? Because it was about John Ashbery."

What the artist wants to direct people to—the erasures in my case, or the way the pencil slid on the surface, the kind of energy in the work, the ability to make a feature come forward—she wasn't directed to that at all. She saw this face and what it seemed to imply—the kind of depth that she saw in it. And I'm thinking to myself, is that the difference between the nonartist person and the art person.

Portrait of John Ashbery, 1953

Portrait of Kenneth Koch, 1953

Here's Kenneth Koch who posed in front of a work of mine, obviously out of my de Kooning period—a little bit of the de Kooning women, I think.

Kenneth Koch and I have known each other many, many years. Of all my friends, he is a rather odd and I would say, difficult personality. He is one of those people you have a social and emotional attachment with from the past, but who you see now mainly through professional connections and you feel sad about it. You get older, you don't see each other every day the way you used to when you didn't know who you were and you had a lot of energy to bounce around all over town. Every so often Kenneth Koch would complete a book and want me to do a cover or do illustrations, and since I always had respect for his talent and thought he was quite funny, I found it a pleasure to do something for him. He has a response to words that is odd and unique. And he even wrote plays in which every so often I would be able to take a part. But finally it became almost only that—the only time he got in touch was when he had some project in mind, and I began to find myself wondering what the whole thing was about. It became very complicated. On the other hand, I consider him one of my closest friends, and here I am doing the jacket for his new book of poems.

Joan Mitchell in a Summer Hat, 1955

Frank O'Hara with Hammer, 1955

Now this is a very important drawing for me since it is a drawing of Frank O'Hara. It has some sort of Christ-like feeling. I even put that Giotto aura around his head. I think I thought of him as Christ in a very funny way and that's why I made him into a carpenter with a hammer. I drew him so many times.

When I drew this I was still interested in getting a leg, and I'd get a few details of the shoe like the buttons and the stripes in the stockings. I did only one eye, but that was something I was already doing. Later in the sixties I began to think that the features and the details aren't as important as certain kinds of groupings of shapes. But I'm very disappointed with this drawing. It looks like a child to me, not a man in his late twenties.

What was Frank's influence on me? Well, I was older than he, so it went the other way. By the time he came to New York I was already an artist, and so he had a certain kind of interest in me. I think his influence on me was that he made me aware of poetry in a certain way. I mean I wanted to read certain things because of him. I was also forced in his presence to try to clarify what I meant by things. Because I had such a good audience, I would try to be more exact or more heroic. I took myself more seriously. He had that effect on me.

He was also gay and he thought he loved me. We slept with each other. I sort of thought, well, I'm straight, but I'm doing this. Well, I don't know how straight I was if I was doing this. And we carried on for a very long time. He was kind of upset; he usually picks on guys who also like women—the classic case of the homosexual who likes "men": by definition a "man" is someone who likes women. So it was a tragic thing, but it straightened out.

I'd give him my house for the summer sometimes if I went abroad. The funny thing was that he would come out to see me for years and years and years. He'd poke his head in late at night and say, "Want a blow job?" Here we are really, getting on, you know, graying at the temples—and he still continued.

There was a painter called Ad Reinhardt who thought that talking about all these things about life and mixing it up with art was just hocum. Ad Reinhardt was a wonderful character who thought that there wasn't anything lower, there wasn't anything more ludicrous, there wasn't anything more embarassing than the relationship between a work of art and the story like the one we're going into now. What has my going to bed with Frank O'Hara got to do with the moment that I'm standing in front of my canvas or a piece of paper with a pencil or a brush?

And actually, he's right in a certain way. He was against people who had all these "interesting" things to say and what was interesting started to become a cliché—like how much *pain* the artist felt, or what he went through, how many drafts he made of a certain drawing. It's like they're living out a drama that Reinhardt found to be ridiculous. On the other hand, look what Ad Reinhardt ended up doing. Ad Reinhardt ended up doing black paintings in which, if you really look very hard, you might be able to find a little dark brown. He worked as hard as he could to eliminate as much rhetoric as he could, and all you're left with is feeling the presence of brown and black.

When we talk about art, we can't help but talk about its relationship to life. There are all sorts of experiences—personal experiences, aesthetic experiences—which are ways of looking at things and coming away from them. It's true that if a person comes over to a painting and the only thing he can say is "Gee, that looks like Aunt Mae's house on Cape Cod," there does seem to be something inferior there to someone who says, "Oh, I like the way he put the yellow down," or "There was a certain kind of drawing in this." We feel as if the experience of art has to do with how the artist handles colors and where he places them on a piece of canvas, things like that. On the other hand, that's inside—that's like the artist's way of looking at it. What of people who don't carry that? How do they look at it?

I don't think that I'm ever leaving myself out. More than others I may be saying something about the individual who's in the work, in some way.

Frank O'Hara Seated, Hands Clasped, 1956

HOW TO PROCEED IN THE ARTS

A detailed study of the creative act

by Larry Rivers and Frank O'Hara

1955

1. Empty yourself of everything.

2. Think of faraway things.

3. It is 12:00. Pick up the adult and throw it out of bed. Work should be done at your leisure, you know, only when there is nothing else to do. If anyone is in bed with you, they should be told to leave. You can not work with someone there.

4. If you're the type of person who thinks in words—paint!

5. Think of a big color—who cares if people call you Rothko. Release your childhood. Release it—

6. Do you hear them say painting is action? We say painting is the timid appraisal of yourself by lions.

7. They say your walls should look no different than your work, but that is only a feeble prediction of the future. We know the ego is the true maker of history, and if it isn't, it should be no concern of yours.

8. They say painting is action. We say, remember your enemies and nurse the smallest insult. Introduce yourself as Delacroix. When you leave, give them your wet crayons. Be ready to admit that jealousy moves you more than art. They say action is painting. Well, it isn't, and we all know abstract expressionism and pop art has moved to the suburbs.

9. If you are interested in schools, choose a school that is interested in you. Cézanne agrees with us when he says "Schools are for fools." We are too embarrassed to decide on the proper approach. However, this much we have observed: good or bad schools are insurance companies. Enter their offices and you are certain of a position. No matter how we despise them, the Pre-Raphaelites are here to stay.

10. Don't just paint. Be a successful all-round man like Baudelaire.

11. Remember to despise your teachers, or for that matter anyone who tells you anything straight from the shoulder. This is very important. For instance, by now you should have decided we are a complete waste of time, Easterners, Communists, and Jews. This will help you with your life, and we have always said "life before art." All other positions have drowned in the boring swamp of dedication. No one makes art because they choose to.

12. If there is no older painter you admire, work twice as much yourself and soon you will be him.

13. Youth wants to burn the museums. We are in them—now what? Better destroy the odors of the zoo. How can we paint the elephants and hippopotamuses? How are we to fill the large empty canvas at the end of the large empty loft? You do have a loft, don't you, man?

14. Is it the beauty of the ugly that haunts the young painter? Does formality encompass all the roaring citadels of the imagination? Aren't we sick of sincerity? We tell you, stitch and draw—fornicate and hate it. We're telling you to begin. Begin! Begin anywhere. Perhaps somewhere in the throat of your loud asshole of a mother? OK? How about some red orange globs mashed into your teacher's daily and unbearable condescension. Try something that pricks the air out of a few popular semantic balloons groping, essence, flat catalyst, crumb, pure painting. How do you feel about titles like "Innscape," "Norway Nights and Suburbs," "No. 188, 1959, Red and a Little Brown," "Hey Mama Baby," "Mandala," and "Still Life with Nose." Even if it is a small work, say 6 feet by 9 feet, it is a start. If it is only as big as a postage stamp, call it a collage—but begin.

15. In attempting a black painting, know that the truth is beauty, but shit is shit.

16. In attempting a figure painting, consider that no amount of distortion will make a painting seem more relaxed. Others must be convinced before we even recognize ourselves. At the beginning, identity is a dream. At the end, it is a nightmare.

17. Don't be nervous. All we painters hate women; unless we hate men.

18. Hate animals and birds. Painting is through with them.

19. When involved with abstractions, refrain, as much as possible, from personal symbolism, unless your point is gossip. . . . Everyone knows size counts.

20. When asked about the Old Masters, be sure to include your theories of culture change, and how the existence of a work of art is only a small part of man's imagination. The Greeks colored their statues, the Spaniards slaughtered their bulls, the Germans invented *Hasenpfeffer*, we dream and act impatient, hoping for fame without labor, admiration without a contract, sex *with* an erection.

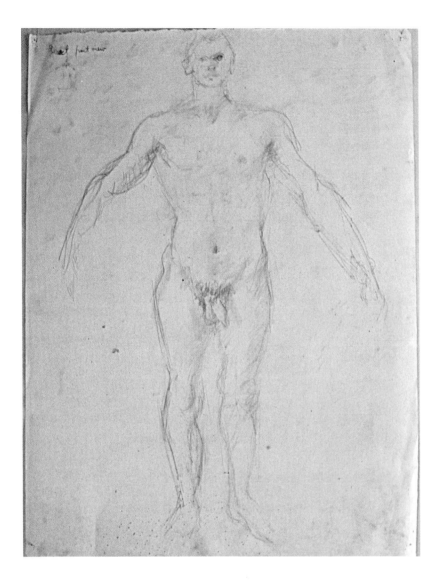

Study of *Frank O'Hara* for sculpture *The Swimmer*, c.1955

Study of *Frank O'Hara* for sculpture *The Swimmer*, c.1955

Every time brings up envies and irritations. There are certain things in the air that are annoying—a certain kind of politician today, certain kinds of rhetoric that you hear on TV. You don't always piece it together, but you know it as soon as you're listening to it. It's cant and it's awful. Well, there was a lot of that in the art world. And Frank and I, we made fun of it—older ideologies, things that were accepted, were valid, were good. We'd stick out our tongues—but in what we thought was an interesting way. I don't think that we ever—either of us—thought that we were about "a better world" or anything like that; or that by getting rid of bullshit we were brightening this lovely universe. But at the same time there was a pleasure asso-

ciated with what we were doing. Aren't we happy with all these beautiful, brilliant, dopey things we're saying? . . .

Once we were invited to a Brown University graduation. It was about 1966, the son of a collector, Jacques Kaplan, was graduating; and we went up there, were put into caps and gowns, given honorary degrees and at the same time we delivered one of these dopey things that we made up for the occasion. There were maybe 3,000 students and we just read. We were talking about homosexuality, fucking, sucking, buggering, art. It predated the unrest on the campus, but it was so in the mood for the students. It was what they liked hearing. We were a great success.

Frank and I enjoyed going out into a certain kind of territory and just reaching into ourselves for all sorts of information that we had. We did a lot of reading of twentieth-century literature, a lot of criticism, art criticism. In fact, Frank finally found out so much he became the curator at the Museum of Modern Art. He started out there selling postcards for Christmas. He got to know so many artists and so much about art and what was going on in the art world that he became completely invaluable to the Museum and finally he was given the job of curator—my version of Horatio O'Hara.

Frank O'Hara, Two Blue Eyes, c. 1955

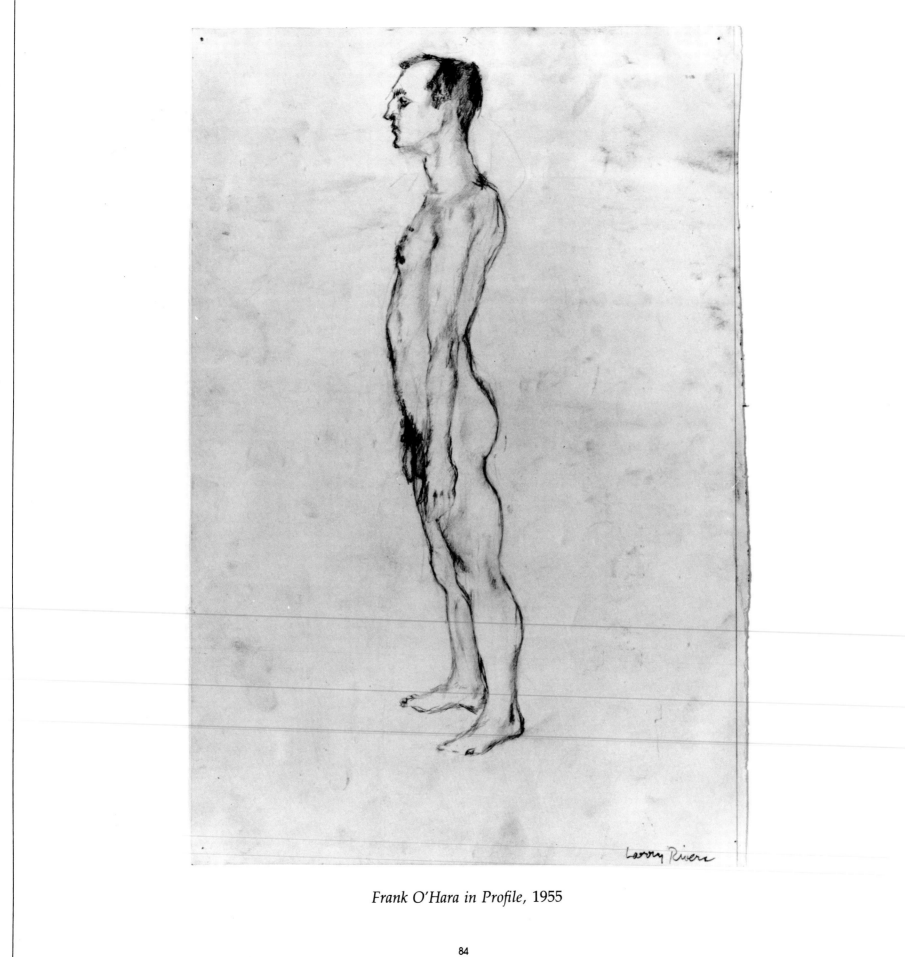

Frank O'Hara in Profile, 1955

This is the drawing for a painting. When this painting was shown in the middle fifties at the Whitney, guards were stationed in front of it to see that it wasn't damaged, that nobody wrote anything on it. There's something about the male nude that is more of a problem than the female nude.

Frank O'Hara with Boots On, study for painting *O'Hara*, 1954

John Myers Going under the Pencil, 1957

Here's John Myers. He looks like Oscar Wilde. He was the gallery dealer at Tibor deNagy who was gay and was in love with me. I drew a lot of him.

"John Myers managed to get me money, he managed to get me a certain amount of attention. He kept my work in the public eye. He would get me commissions for paintings, decor for stage, illustrating for poets. People began to pay attention to me. But as time goes on your needs change and the people you surround yourself with change, too. The kind of personal dealer Myers was, which was very important for the artists and the art scene of the fifties and the early sixties was not what I wanted later. I was wrong. I say that today. An artist needs nurturing all his life. Even on an aesthetic level he was helpful with just the right touch of insanity necessary for me to keep mine.

I didn't understand that. I was cocky and ambitious. I left him in the lurch." —*Newsday*

This is an early drawing of Martha Jackson, and she looks like she's in a fireman's hat. Nor does it look like Martha Jackson. Martha Jackson was a gallery dealer who was one of the first to come out and make deals with me. And I was your artist willing to make deals. I didn't have any guilt about it. It was the money and the action. You make something, a dealer buys it, puts it up for sale, someone else buys it; the dealer makes money, comes back for more—I'm in the world hanging on someone's wall. What else was I about? What else would give me pleasure?

Martha Jackson as a Fireman, 1953

Grace Hartigan is a painter I knew in the fifties. She was really a funny girl, spoke all day about painting and what she's doing; she tried to connect herself to the masters. I did that too—like if I did something of a Cézanne or a Delacroix, maybe some of their greatness would rub off on me. We thought she was funny because of her poses; it was as if she were in some kind of costume all the time, a costume of attitudes. But she was an important figure. She did all sorts of odd things in her time with men that were interesting. She'd run off with one and then three weeks later she'd be with another. Today it's nothing.

Before she became Grace Hartigan she was "George Hartigan." And then slowly she began to be "G. Hartigan" and then finally Grace. She was certainly some kind of female equivalent of a rough-and-ready type. . . . I think now that time has passed I realize what these women were up against. I sort of accepted them just as guys or as another person—I didn't think about it too much. But they had to be quite strong and maybe even exaggerate their position to keep from going under, but at the same time, the "man" part seemed to be as important as ever. . . . Men seem to think that they can make a separation between career and the emotional/sexual aspect of life. Until recently women kept thinking that somehow they had to settle the man thing; somehow it was paramount. That wasn't true for Grace, I think; she was just as interested in a career, in her work, and men were like dressing—a little bit of spice in life. She seemed to boss them around—like, "Don't bother me, I'm doing my work, you can call between five and six. . . ." That would seem very normal today. Everybody is alone.

Her paintings were very forceful and full of bravado and at the same time there wasn't too much content. At one point I think she envisioned that she was going to conquer the world with her painting—we all did. Then she made a decision about a certain man, a Mr. Price, who was a scientist who was going to discover a cure for the common cold. She married and moved to Baltimore with him and thought that even in the anonymity of Baltimore her greatness would shine, and I'm afraid that reality had a rude shock for her. I think she survived like we all do—I don't care what happens, you don't throw yourself on the pyre . . . . I saw her a few years ago down in Baltimore. She's in pretty good shape; she works hard. I don't know how much attention the public has paid to her, but she has shows all over the country. She's OK.

Grace came from a kind of middle-class Irish background with certain pretensions, and I think this drawing catches some of that. You know that kind of thing that lingers with women—like their taste in clothes? They just learn it from their mothers and they can change their whole life and everything, but when they walk into that store they're still that same person. There's something about the way they go and get a blouse or a pair of shoes. I can never do it. I have got to go with someone—I can't buy clothes by myself. I can't make up my mind what I look like or what I want to look like. I'm a patsy for every girl that I go with; any idea that they have of me is OK with me. . . . I went with a certain girl who wanted me to be some kind of Brooks Brothers type; I tried it for a while, it was a laugh. Way back in the early fifties, on my own, I decided I was the thrift shop type and bought all my clothes in a thrift-shop—trolley-car conductor outfits, Russian boots, the works. The idea of spraying my boots with metallic paint came from preserving them after they got chewed up in 1957 when I was welding. That isn't a fashion thing, it's an occupational thing. I always thought it was a good idea to protect shoes that looked like they were dying. . . . But Grace Hartigan, as for her, there was always a certain classic "look" that stuck.

Portrait of Grace Hartigan, c.1956

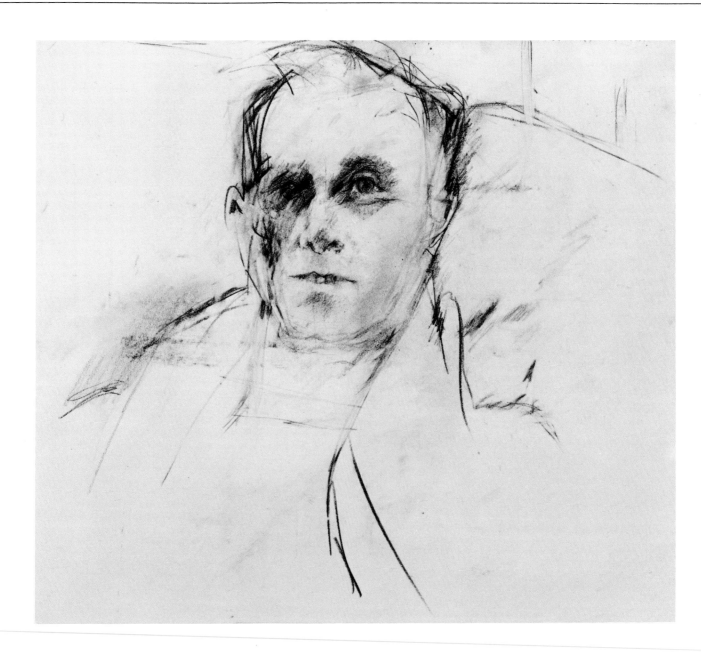

Portrait of Edwin Denby III, 1953

Edwin Denby was a dancer and a dance critic with the *Herald Tribune* when I met him, but he's actually a poet and a very aesthetic man and I would say the closest person to that pure type I was speaking of. He still lives in a very spare-looking loft on Twenty-first Street. I lived there once myself in the late forties. He's been living there since maybe the thirties, forties. It's the only building standing on that street. And he's a white-haired man now.

He's a man who might have good cause to be bitter. I don't think he's been given the recognition he de-serves. He's a very smart man, very sensitive—he was there when everything was happening—but it seems as if whatever constitutes worldly recognition hasn't come to him. On the other hand, among his friends he's got a great reputation. He's well liked and he's looked up to. He's a little bit like a guru. I think that John Ashbery once complained about that—about how he dispensed his approval: the world didn't rec-ognize him, but he knew his power, his group.

He was sick in Southampton and lying in bed when I made this drawing. He's a strange person. I never was sure whether he liked me or not. I always respected him and he had a certain distance to you in friendship. But, on the other hand, Frank O'Hara and he were close. Frank seems to have been able to reach him.

He's from a rather old American family from Kansas, I think, and people of his were admirals in the Navy. I've always considered him to be a real American, while I am a fake American—sort of American by mistake. After all, my mother came here when she was twenty-six, my father was fourteen; and all I saw were foreigners in my house, and I spoke Yiddish till I was six years old. . . . That's not in the drawing. The drawing is like all the drawings I did at that time, but all those thoughts passed through my head as I did him. . . . Actually, when I think about it now, the thing about America is that I don't think anybody feels like an "American." And the ones that do—the "real" Americans from English-Scottish backgrounds —are a dying race. The country is inhabited by everyone but Americans. There's a cohesiveness in other countries, in Germany, England. But America is strange in that way.

EAT—Portrait of Joseph LeSueur, 1961

Head of Molly Adams, 1957

Molly Adams. She was like a first girl friend. I don't remember having one before except for Jane Freilicher, who was way back and then I had a long period of homosexuality, a little bestiality, a little of this and that and drugs. And then I started seeing Molly around 1956. She was a waitress out in the Hamptons. I was playing sax with a group in a place called the Elm Tree—she came by. She was quite beautiful and very different from me; she was Miss Adams; she could trace her ancestry back to the Adamses. Later she became kind of a fanatic about "her country." She acted as if America belonged to her and the rest of us were all foreigners and Jews.

She was always sick. She was the first one I knew who was into Reichian therapy. She would sit in the orgone box and then she would put on an orgone shawl. She was perfect for me because she never wanted to go anywhere at night, so I used to go out at night and stay out very late and she was like a mother in a certain way. I mean, Momma's always there. I'd go out and have fun, do my drugs, music, whatever, and she would be there. . . . She was interested in my art insofar as I was someone she was with. Now she claims she knew all along I was a genius.

It's strange that I put in two eyes that time—I rarely put in two eyes. Somewhere along the line I figured out that you get the look of a person better if you only do one. You have to place the second one really quite accurately; otherwise it looks peculiar. Given that I wasn't that interested in realism, it seemed to me to be intelligent to have left the other out. Finally, I just began leaving them out because I was used to leaving them out.

This is Bob Thompson who was an artist. He was around in the fifties and sixties. We used to do heroin together. He died pretty young. Don't ask me how. He got sick.

Head of Bob Thompson, 1960

93

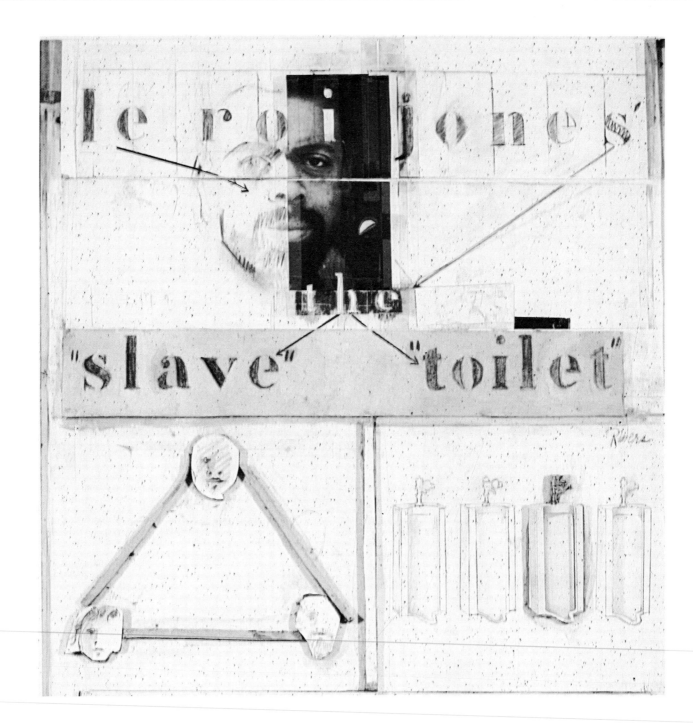

"The Toilet" and *"The Slave,"* finish for poster for the two one-act plays by LeRoi Jones, 1964

LeRoi Jones, the Cisco Kid, he was a friend of mine. In the late fifties, early sixties, he was my connection to a lot of things. He was black and he was interested in jazz, or he was interested in jazz and happened to be black. He was a nice guy. We got on drugs together and we went to parties together and we did all sorts of things together. He married a white Jewish girl and I got him a house out in the Hamptons and made sure

there weren't going to be any question about him being a black man.

Then after 1964, after his play *The Dutchman* was produced, suddenly it all changed. We were invited to a symposium on I don't know what—"art *vs.* life," some funny thing—and suddenly he decided to come out of some kind of closet with the most intense hatred of every white person he knew. It was the beginning of those very aggressive black/white situations. I couldn't believe it. I was shocked and upset, and that began the deterioration in our friendship. Finally, he told me I was just painting for a bunch of uptown fags. He's come off it a bit like all of us do with time. He's changed his name to Imamu Amiri Baraka, and now Imamu is a devoted Marxist, and I've heard that he writes plays and directs them to educate

black students in Marxism. Very strange, he's liable to become something else again.

These are drawings I did when LeRoi Jones asked me to do the sets for two short plays *The Toilet* and *The Slave*. From the point of view of drawing, these are the beginning of my more three-dimensional things.

Portrait of LeRoi Jones, study for poster for the one-act plays *The Toilet* and *The Slave,* 1964

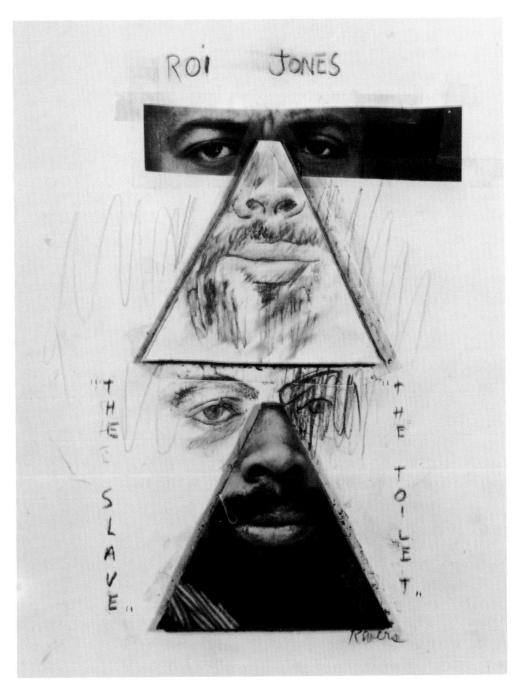

Portrait of Bob Stone Torso, 1953

Bob Stone was an artist who left home at fourteen and whose story interested me. He also got drugs for me in the fifties. He thought he painted like Gorky and I thought so too. I haven't heard from him in years. This drawing catches something—a kind of refinement. A strangely delicate man.

I drew this one summer in the Hamptons. The guy is out at my summer place. He's hanging around—somewhere along the line I'll say, "Well, why don't you sit down?" I'm identifying myself as an artist every time I do this, right? The more you do it, the more it means you mean it. The more you mean it, the more someone accepts the idea. It's a syndrome you can't escape. And then you want it. Artists are so peculiar—they have to be "identified" over and over. On the other hand, the nature of the activity is that it does take a long time to do *anything*, so you have to be doing it all the time. My work may be more novelistic than certain poetic-painters who paint in a rush of feeling, get something out, then *pffffft!*—lie exhausted. My thing is quite different. I don't have that.

Announcement of exhibition at the Tibor de Nagy Gallery, 1956

Portrait of Ornette Coleman, illustration for Ronald Firbank's *New Rhythm*, 1963

Jack Teagarden and Trombone, cover for Columbia Records, 1960

Gregory Corso as an Electric Fan, 1959

Gregory Corso was a Beat poet along with Jack Kerouac and Allen Ginsberg, and we were all thrown together, we saw each other quite a bit. The beat poets were quite different from Frank and John and Kenneth who probably without saying it, considered themselves aristocrats. These poets considered themselves the poets of the people, or the poets of the lost souls of the world. They identified more with the junkies or the poets who had hard times. They had a different romance, the beat poets, than the romance that, say, John Ashbery and Kenneth and Frank had. But at the same time so much attention was paid to them that the others were forced to acknowledge their existence. Allen Ginsberg is the only one of the beats who has really survived, but the way the world turned out,

Allen is more acknowledged for his notoriety and political positions than his poetry, and I think he suffers a little bit because of it.

This is a portrait of Gregory Corso as a "fan." His hands are joined—again there's that trick of mine where I wouldn't put the fingers in. I just made the shape of the wrist to wrist—from where the shirt stops on one hand, through the fingers, to the other fingers, up to the wrist where there's another sleeve—and that would always form some sort of shape. To unravel those digits that are crossing, to keep track of the fingers—I finally got bored with that and just had a different thing in mind. You can see now that it's all one piece.

Gregory Corso is now married to an heiress—really

a rich woman, and it's insane. I knew him when he had gotten out of jail and was wearing it like a badge—"I was in jail, I'm one of those wonderful poets." He was a big druggie and a *bon vivant*. He ran after women, considered himself a hedonist, a baller, see—then he lost all his teeth. No one paid much attention to his work, although he really was interested in his poetry. I mean through all the fuss and the kind of fun he would have—he acted like a fool always, you know—underneath there was always a very serious interest in his work. Then he was taken seriously. I think he taught in universities, but he kept himself in this awful state. I mean, no teeth; he lived in Chelsea; he wanted to look like his clothes stunk. But there are still women who want to be associated with that, and finally he hooked up with someone—can't remember which fortune—it's as heavy as Du Pont. So we all travel on strange roads all our lives. I'm fond of him when I see him. He's so sweet now that it forces you to be, you know, nicer.

Relaxed, c. 1959

Maxine, 1959

In 1958 Maxine was "my girl friend." I called her Miss New Jersey. Maxine Groffsky, who was the subject matter for the character Brenda in Philip Roth's *Goodbye Columbus.* We kept up a relationship—then she became angry with me.

This drawing was done out in a barn in Southampton. She had a beautiful nose—and even though the drawing is quite abstract, you can see that I was aware of her nose with these two dots. I was very aware of it because I've thought about a nose job since I was eighteen. I mean you live in a culture where everybody's nose is going up, or is straight, and you walk around looking like some Arab or an anti-Semitic notion of an Elder of Zion—well, you sort of consider it. At any rate, by now, what are you going to do? My sister had a nose job. It always made me nervous.

Miss New Jersey, Portrait of Maxine Groffsky, 1959

Female Karl Marx, 1959

Naomi Levine. This girl was like a pal. You know how you sort of make a silent decision about almost everybody you come into contact with? Would you, wouldn't you? Do you want to, don't you? There's nothing you can do about it; it's annoying almost. With this girl I made up my mind, no. But she would come to see me, so it would always be "No, but. . . ."

I must have named this drawing later in the sixties when I was doing the *History of the Russian Revolution.* It had nothing to do with her—except perhaps that like Karl Marx she had that kind of lion's head, heavy.

Here we have a drawing where I've completely lost interest in what's there in front of me. I'm creating very peculiar rectangles and swirls and sweeps and swooshes, using the body to allow me to do this.

I don't know what to call this, but I'll tell you what it is. I found a girl outside my doorway one night very drunk, and I took her in and let her sleep in the studio. When she woke up in the morning I started to draw her. She wasn't very attractive—actually a sort of female hobo, but she was young. I thought it was kind of romantic and I drew her.

This is one of the girls I don't remember. I was like those English painters who used to go out and try to find beautiful girls and bring them back. It was very eighteenth century of me. If the subject was beautiful, if you brought her to your studio and got her to pose, it was like "Art holds a mirror up to nature," that idea.

Girl, c.1959

De Kooning with My Texas Hat, 1963

This is a drawing of Bill de Kooning in a hat that I picked up at a shop in San Antonio, Texas. I think it dated back to the National Recovery Act because it had an NRA label on it. I was in love with it for a long time. . . . Anyway, Bill came over to my house drunk one afternoon, trying to make out with Ellen Oppen-

heim. I don't know whether he succeeded. As I look back at it now, he would show up drunk over the years, and usually with a woman and usually in a fight—and he was a very aggressive and boring drunk, really quite intolerable. But this time I remember I just plunked this hat on him and made him sit while I did a drawing of him. I don't know, he had some curious vanities. He was very good-looking—he still is actually, white-haired and everything.

Even though my works had begun to change from the point of view of realism, I reverted here to a very strict attempt at getting what he looked like. In this case the two eyes and even the rendition of the hat is quite accurate, with the curves and the twists and the

Portrait of Willem de Kooning III, 1963

dents. You can see I tried to even get part of his stubble which after two, three days of drinking had begun to grow; being a kind of northern European his beard doesn't look heavy, although it was heavy. Anyway, that's Bill de Kooning.

I must say that I have done several versions of this drawing. Lots of people wanted to buy it, and instead of being your very honest and sincere artist, I did what Rodin did.

Full Figure of Willem de Kooning, 1961

Wiped Out, Portrait of Willem de Kooning, 1961

There he is again. It's the same day, I believe. Here he looks more vulnerable and you can see that I probably didn't like his nose. You know what that nose is composed of in the first drawing, and here I find that I must not have liked it, or not gotten it structurally satisfying, and so I tend to erase it, erase it, erase it, keep trying, erase, keep trying, erase, and finally in this case, I figured, well, let the observer make up more than I can represent. Sometimes a certain kind of paper won't give up a mark, so you just have the remains. This drawing is in the tradition of those kinds of work in which the history of the work became part of the quality of the work. De Kooning's work is full of that. His whole genre is that. His work is all about sweeping away, putting in . . . struggle, struggle, struggle and poof—masterpiece!!!

De Kooning is an interesting man. I went for long walks with him. I talked with him. He was like a soul father to me and yet a very harassed man, so it wasn't that he was so complacent and so well placed in the world, you know. He wasn't like that. He was a sufficiently older artist for me so that I respected his opinions and I had a certain pleasure in walking with him and talking. We did that all the time late at night. And actually we came to be quite close, and it still remains. I don't see him that much now, but I could call and go see him. As an older friend he wouldn't get in touch with me, but he's always glad to see me.

The Last Civil War Veteran—Dead, 1961

THE LAST CONFEDERATE SOLDIER

It's sort of poignant, you know. The next to last Civil War veteran died—it was St. Patrick's Day, 1959, and he was a one-hundred-and-twelve-year-old man. About ten, fifteen years before his death, he was made into an honorary general and he used to sit on his porch in his uniform; people would pass by his house down in Tennessee, and they would salute him. I did a painting of him.

Then once this "next-to-the-last" confederate soldier died, there was this one guy left from the Civil War. Now he was a media thing immediately: the *last* Civil War veteran. So I began getting interested in *him* and I did paintings. Then he died. They started to look up his records and it turned out that maybe he lied— and the guy who was supposed to be the "next-to-the-last" was actually the last. But this was covered up—and Mr. Walter Williams, I believe his name was, was buried with honors. This *Last Civil War Veteran* was

done from a photograph that appeared in *Life* magazine: the vet in his coffin and a Marine guard. When it appeared, Ray Parker, the artist, sent it to me with a note reading " Go!" He wanted me to do something with it, make a painting of it. He knew that somehow this had become a subject of mine.

Ten years later I was commissioned by Florists Transworld Delivery to do something with flowers and I did a three-dimensional version of the dead civil war veteran with a bouquet. By then I knew why I had jumped at the subject visually. It was all about death, and there were all those ironies— an old man buried by the state, a relic of past glories. For this last piece I talked Campbell's Funeral Chapel into selling me a coffin—no mean feat if you don't happen to be an undertaker. Then I had the delightful experience of seeing myself in a coffin; I had the upper part of my own body cast as the dead veteran.

This is the end of a long series I did on the last Civil War veteran. I had done them in the United States, but I was in Europe in 1961 when I did this one. I had just gotten one of those air-mail European letters that you fold, you know, and the page you write on becomes the envelope, and I used that gray. The color was the gray-blue of the uniform, so I just laid it out.

"End of the Gallant Rebs," *Life* magazine photograph, January 11, 1960

The Last Civil War Veteran—Dead, 1961

The Last Civil War Veteran—Dead, 1961

Four of a series of twelve *Stones*, verses by Frank O'Hara, 1958

F I V E

COLLABORATIONS AND ILLUSTRATIONS

As a younger painter, I had the notion that there was an intrinsic good in painters and poets working together. It seemed like socialism in its smallest and most personal form. I had the idea that the assault on the senses coming from two directions, pictorial and poetic, would be twice as strong. "Ya got da woids and da pichers." There was a glorious halo around the idea of inspiring the other.

My chance came along in the summer of 1957 when Tanya Grosman started her lithography studio and asked me to do a series of stones with Frank O'Hara. How were two superserious, monstrously developed egos going to find a way of allowing an undiluted exposition of their talents? We just tried it; our ignorance and enthusiasm allowed us to jump into it without thinking about the details and difficulties.

The lithograph stone surface is very smooth. The marks going on it are made with a rubbery, difficult-to-handle crayon or with a dark liquid called tusche. I had never seen any of this equipment before, and unless I was thinking about Picasso or Matisse, I thought of printmaking as the dull occupation of pipe-smoking, corduroy-jacket-type artisans. Technically,

it was a cumbersome task. Whatever you do on a stone comes out opposite to the way you put it down. It is almost impossible to erase, one of my more important crutches. To change something requires scraping it off the stone with a razor. One needed the patience of another age, but we kept doing it whenever my calendar of events and his fused into a free afternoon or evening.

Each time we got together, we would choose some very definite subject, and since there was nothing we had more access to than ourselves, the first stone was called *Us*. The title always came first. It was the only way we could get started. He'd write something, and with his charged breath on my neck to make something, I would think "What can I use in his words to continue?" I never entertained the idea of matching the mood of his words. It was always some specific object. Then he took what I did and either commented on it with his words or took it somewhere else in any way he felt like doing. If something in the drawing didn't please him, he could alter it by the quality of his words. Frank was almost as important as myself in the overall visual force of the print.

Jack Kerouac, cover illustration for *The Lonesome Traveler* by Jack Kerouac, 1960

This is Jack Kerouac, believe it or not—an attempt for the cover of his book, *The Lonesome Traveler*. We're into the early sixties here and I see I'm leaving out jaws, details. I'm interested in Franz Kline's work, and large, chunky shapes begin to come in, even though I still had to have recognizable subject matter.

I don't know where my direction comes from when I depart from the subject; I don't know what directs me. I've been thinking about the painter Richard Lindner, who died recently, about how clear some people are about what they want to do. For a long time their ideas may seem corny or anachronisms, and then finally we look at them and we think, "My God, what a steadiness of spirit!" Lately, I've been feeling that there are only one or two things that move me—but I don't want to be thought *only* interested in realism or subject matter. Even though you recognize people, things in my work, that isn't my supreme concern. . . . But I jump back and forth. At one moment I may stand up to someone and say, "Well, what the fuck is wrong with subject matter? Maybe that's all that's interesting about it. What do you think art is about? I don't know and you don't know." And at other times I will think, well, there is some kind of truth to the fact that a picture is composed of certain kinds of plastic, abstract things that have to be dealt with—where you place something on a surface what you leave out, texture, form, etc.

I went over to the freight yards on Eleventh Avenue—which still exist actually—and sat down to try to get these freight trains for *The Lonesome Traveler*. It was the middle of winter over fifteen years ago. This is my thing—a little line, a little erasure, a little heavy, a little gray.

Box Cars, illustration for *The Lonesome Traveler* by Jack Kerouac, 1960

Roofs and Cathedral in France, illustration for *The Lonesome Traveler* by Jack Kerouac, 1960

Beat, illustration for *The Lonesome Traveler* by Jack Kerouac, 1960

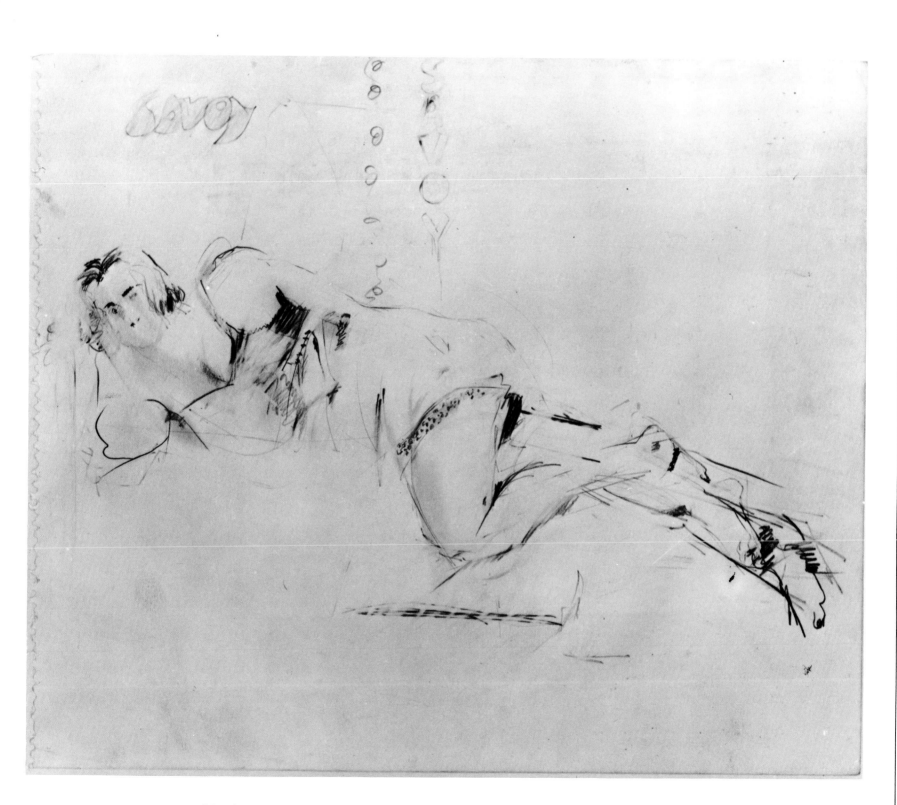

Hotel Room, illustration for *The Lonesome Traveler* by Jack Kerouac, 1960

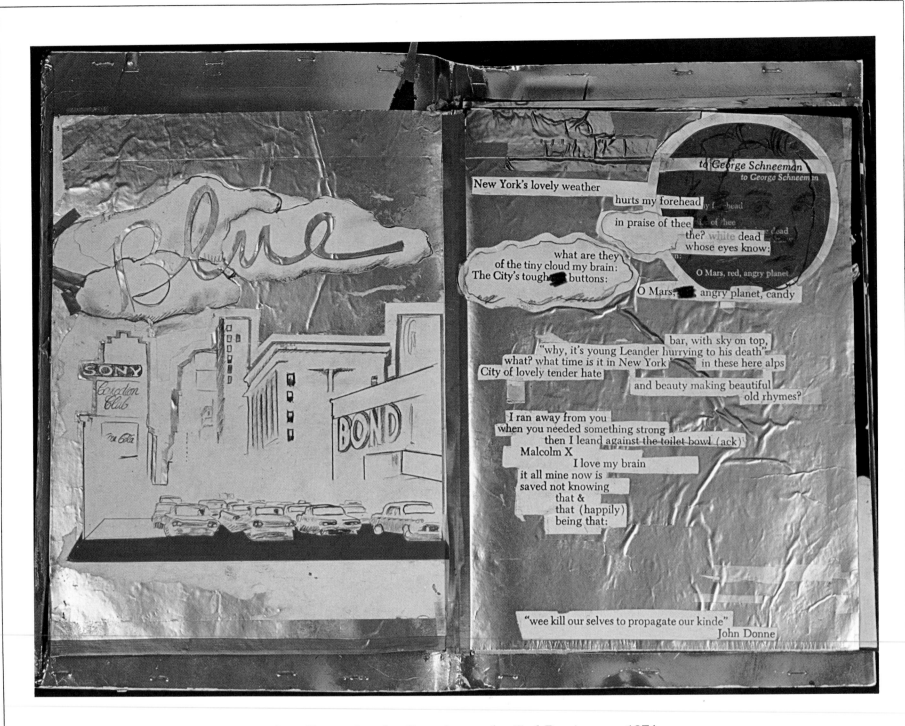

Blue, illustration for *Bean Spasms* by Ted Berrigan, c. 1974

This is from a book I did with the poet Ted Berrigan called *Bean Spasms*. It's lost; someone actually stole it. I have transparencies of all the pages; I'm going to have to reproduce them. This was the best thing I did with vinyl—it was fantastic. The cover was about New York City and some of the pages were cut out of purple vinyl, white vinyl. On the first page shown here there was something about the gold and blue of New York and I just put the word *blue* in the sky.

Ted Berrigan was a kind of disciple of Frank O'Hara. Frank liked him and I met him through Frank and we became friends ourselves. I did illustrations for all the poets, you know, and there was something in this work that I liked.

I enjoy these projects. But if you've grown up in an era where the worst thing you can accuse someone of is doing *illustration*, you wonder. "Well, it has an illustrative quality" was like saying, "It stinks." It was like a snob attitude. Now I take it the other way. I say to myself, I can do illustrations. I feel like I'm an illustrator. I don't mind it—it's exact, a clear term.

Manhattan, illustration for *Bean Spasms* by Ted Berrigan, c.1974

Announcement for poetry reading with Ted Berrigan and Anne Waldmann, c. 1973

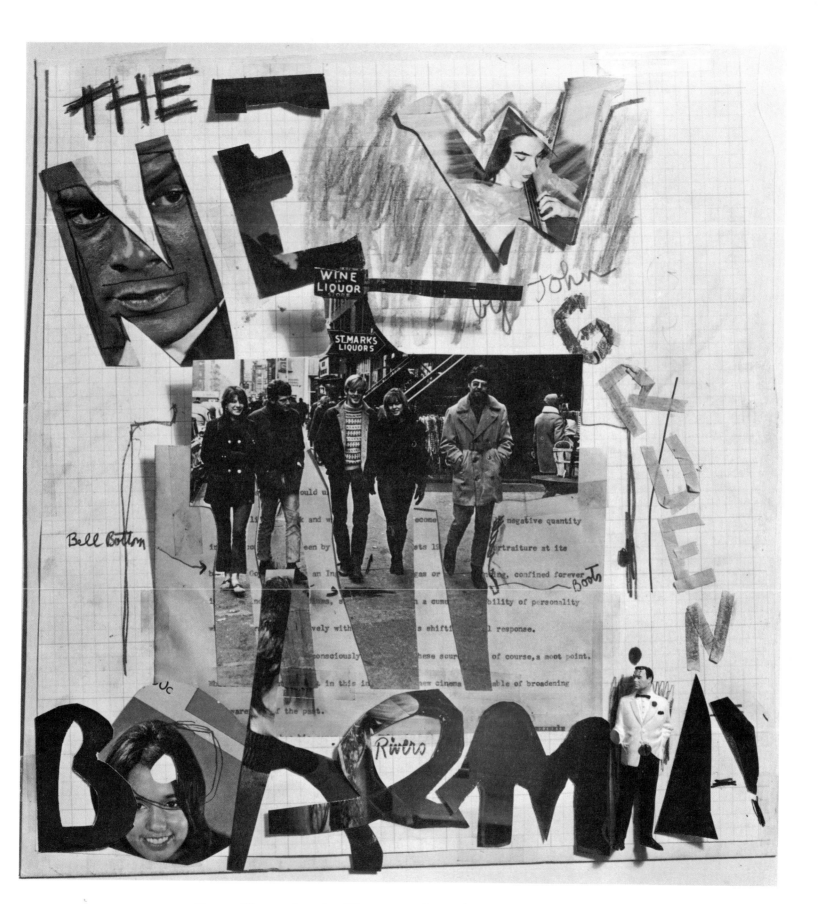

Cover illustration for *The New Bohemia* by John Gruen, 1966

Cover illustration for *When the Sun Tries to Go On* by Kenneth Koch, 1970

Frank, dedication illustration for *When the Sun Tries to Go On* by Kenneth Koch, 1970

A preposterous rhinoceros . . . , illustration for *When the Sun Tries to Go On* by Kenneth Koch, 1970

Animal crowding . . ., illustration for *When the Sun Tries to Go On* by Kenneth Koch, 1970

The dirty beautiful jingling pyjamas . . ., illustration for *When the Sun Tries to Go On* by Kenneth Koch, 1970

This one is from a series I did called *The Ten Commandments, "Thou shalt not covet thy neighbor's wife...."* It was commissioned by a synagogue in Connecticut; the architect was Percy Goodman, brother of the writer, Paul. They're the most abstract things I did, but you can still make out the subject matter—a face with a leering eye, female legs, and two houses. These were going to be translated into little metal pieces outside the wall of the synagogue. But when the congregation saw these sketches and heard me talking about them, I think they decided that they'd stick to the dictum "Thou shalt not commit graven images of thy God." They were never used.

Thou shalt not covet thy neighbors . . . , drawing for *The Ten Commandments*, 1954

thou shalt not covet they neighbors ...

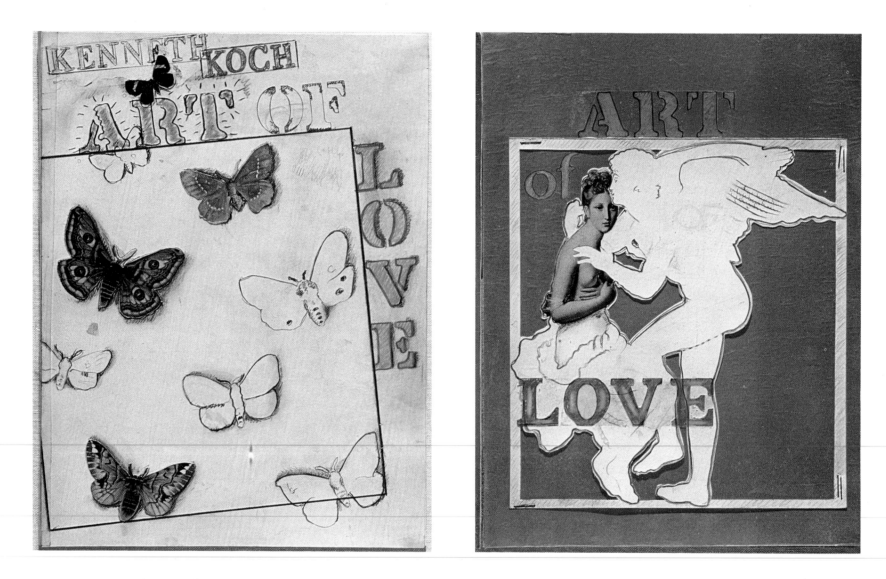

The Art of Love, studies for cover illustration for *The Art of Love* by Kenneth Koch, c.1974

The Art of Love, study for cover illustration for *The Art of Love* by Kenneth Koch, c. 1974

Illustration for *The Donkey and the Darling* by Terry Southern, 1968–77

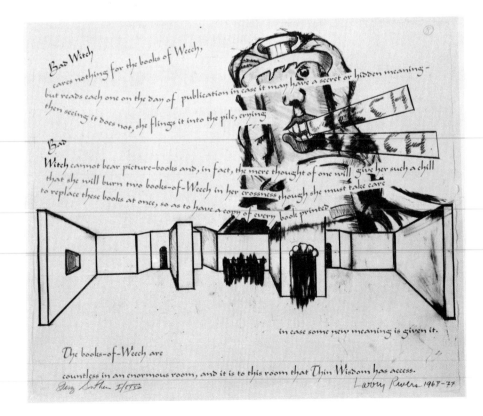

Illustration for *The Donkey and the Darling* by Terry Southern, 1968–77

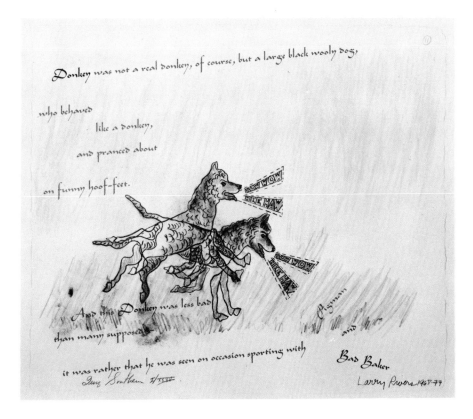

Illustration for *The Donkey and the Darling* by Terry Southern, 1968–77

Illustration for *The Donkey and the Darling* by Terry Southern, 1968–77

For C's 35th, 1974

CLARICE, VOCABULARY LESSONS, FRENCH MONEY

Through familiarity the artist comes to something that he has not previously expressed, like the difference between a one-night stand with someone, where the evening is full of a new and interesting relationship, or something that comes out of knowing someone for a long time, that seems to be more sustaining. In *Remembrance of Things Past,* Proust starts with an acquaintanceship with the details of his own life—not with anything new. His thing was to be so familiar with a remembered event that he could turn it over on its side or on its back for aspects that could only come with great familiarity. I mean, he had a lot to draw on. I think one has greater art who seems to have more than he has shown, not one who has shown most that he has.

These are all Clarice. A Welsh girl, Clarice Price. I did lots of drawings of her. She was an easy subject, willing to pose, and quiet. She knew artists in England. By the time I got to know her, after she came to work for me in New York, she had posed for artists and she didn't seem to have an ego problem about Did it look like me? Did it make me good looking? Did it make me ugly? She didn't have that at all. So she was a

person that I drew a lot. Without thinking about it then, that must have been an attractive quality for an artist who is interested in realism—not to worry about how the person is reacting.

I first met her when she came to New York to work as my maid and to take care of my son, and so for a year she was just someone who worked for me. She had a boyfriend and I had Maxine . . . but it was sort of nice to see her there every day and not be involved sexually—it always gets in the way. She was a happy sort of person, you know, nice she was. I got to know her better really that way, and then we got sexually close and were married.

Around this time I had begun to feel uncomfortable with naturalistic conventions. I still wanted to draw the thing I was looking at, but I began to feel the necessity for something else, some distraction. I wanted you to follow a limb, to see what somebody looked like, and at the same time I wanted you to begin to see that it is actually a drawing—it's about art; it is art. And so I began fitting rectangles around certain parts; I wanted to encase them. Later on Marisol carried this kind of thing further with her boxed-in figures, but this was much earlier, '62 or '63.

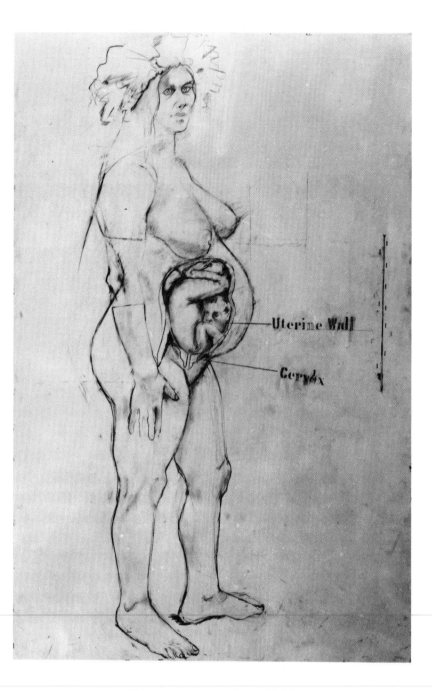

Pregnancy Drawing, 1964

This is the first pregnancy drawing, 1964—still in the collection of the artist I believe. I haven't seen it recently so I wonder where it is, come to think of it. . . . I took a drawing of a uterus that I found in some medical book and put it in. I think that by accident I chose a baby that was in the breech position and it's completely outsized. And I was still doing things with vocabulary lessons, and so here I just named the cervix, uterine wall, and so on. . . . She had her own feather hat on. Quite nice.

Niki de Saint-Phalle traced this drawing a few years later. She reversed it and filled it up with cockamamies—all sorts of things that you could buy. And it still looked quite realistic because of the way she did it. Then she asked if I could do the face.

Here's another portrait of Clarice. It's pencil, crayon, and airbrush on paper. And I'm into that thing again where I'm using rectangles, and here I've even sprayed a template. Again I'm proving to my contemporaries that I'm arrogant about realism. I'm not that interested in it. My interests were varied.

Seated Figure and Templates, c.1965

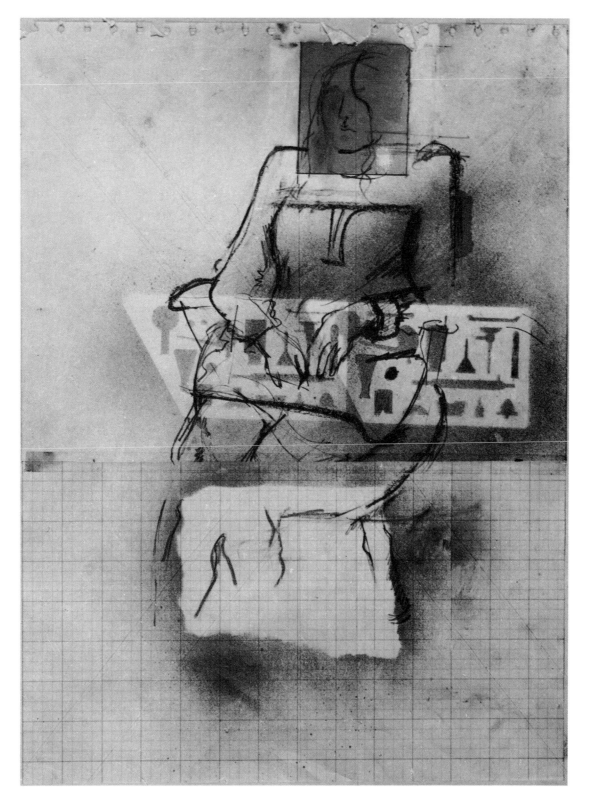

Clarice in a Rectangle, 1961

Clarice in a Hat, 1964

Clarice with Top of Dress Open, 1965–66

This is a view of Clarice Rivers when she is pregnant for the second time.

This is Clarice just before we split in '68. . . . I just took a little part of the design of the dress and then left it. Either I didn't have the concentration for continuing, or I didn't feel it was necessary. It looks like I was in that mood where I thought that the design aspects— the plastic, abstract qualities of the subject—were enough.

Seated Clarice, 1962

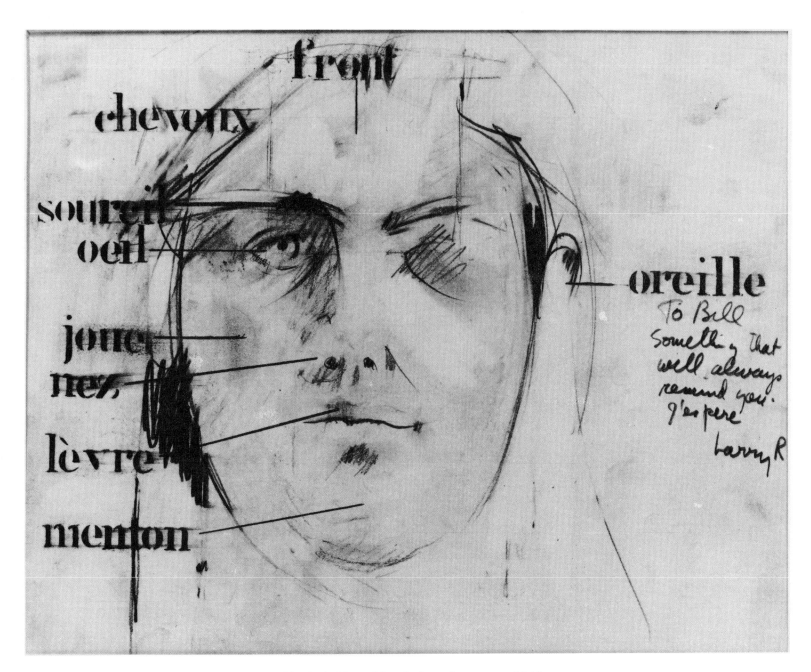

Clarice's Face: Vocabulary Lesson, c. 1962

"The language series grew out of my going to the Alliance Française in Paris. They actually had a lesson book with the face of a rather idiotic-looking boy with lines coming out of the features and a ball at the end of the line with a number on it. The number referred down on the page to the name of the feature. At the bottom of the page, 6 was *'nez'*, 5 was *'bouche,'* etc. It struck me that rather than putting a ball at the end of the line, I could actually put in the word. I stenciled the word, which gives it a kind of manufactured look with a hard edge in contrast to the softer, indefinite lines from my hand." *Newsday*

These works, when I look back now, continue to give me the most pleasure of any work I did in the sixties.

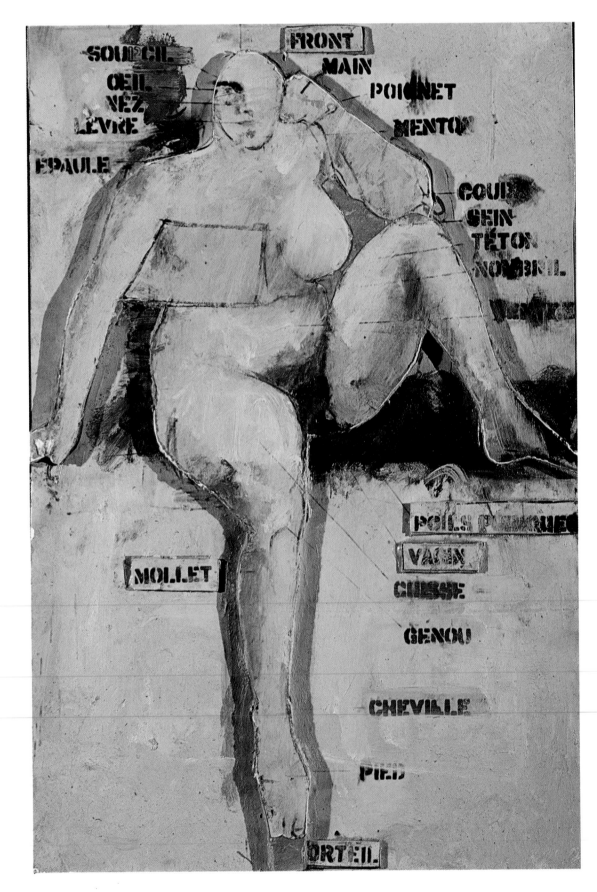

Parts of the Body—French, 1962

I guess my children would characterize me by saying that I didn't spend any time with them. On the other hand, what about men who get up and go out to work every day all day long? At least I was working within eyesight of Gwynne and Emma.

Gwynne and Emma Rivers Carbon Drawing, 1976

For the Marriage of Jane and Joe, 1963

Now here we have a rather poignant one. It's an "epithalamium"—a term I learned from my poet friends—a marriage poem. I had gotten married to Clarice—I may have had marriage on the brain. But the thing is this is my old girl friend who is marrying someone else. By the time I made the drawing ten years after the fact, I was no longer shook up. I *was* kind of shook up when it happened. Not when she married him, but when she ran off with him, and the conditions under which it took place. But she did me the greatest favor that ever happened to anybody—I got sore at her and moved out to the country, to Southampton, and everything started from there.

This is one of the drawings that is really from art books, those books that had bad charcoal reproductions of old masters in them. I started using them in my paintings, like the knee there—if you made a pencil line over it, it could look like your own work. I became completely enamored of these books, and I would not only trace them, I would cut out whole parts of a figure and paste them in. That dress is probably straight from the book. I would take it out, use it like a collage, and then "art it up" so to speak. Juxtaposing four or five pieces from these books—

then adding my own thing is a delightful sort of experience given the kind of humor I have.

You ask whether in some way I was trying to establish the fact that art is always half fakery? Don't forget—when we look back on the work of the Renaissance we attribute it to certain men, but all of them had studios. We don't know which part of the paintings were really painted by the masters.

But the end of this story about *Jane and Joe* is that I'm doing an epithalamium for the girl I was in love with, Jane Freilicher, who married another man. I was obviously nuts at the time that I knew her, and she would have been out of her mind to even think seriously about me. I probably never would have married her, it would have been a complete fiasco. So it's strange. I like her, I see her, she's one of my better friends, and I feel affection for her and her husband. Anyway, that's *Jane and Joe.*

Portrait of Joe Hazan, c.1961

A Dream of Botticelli, 1963

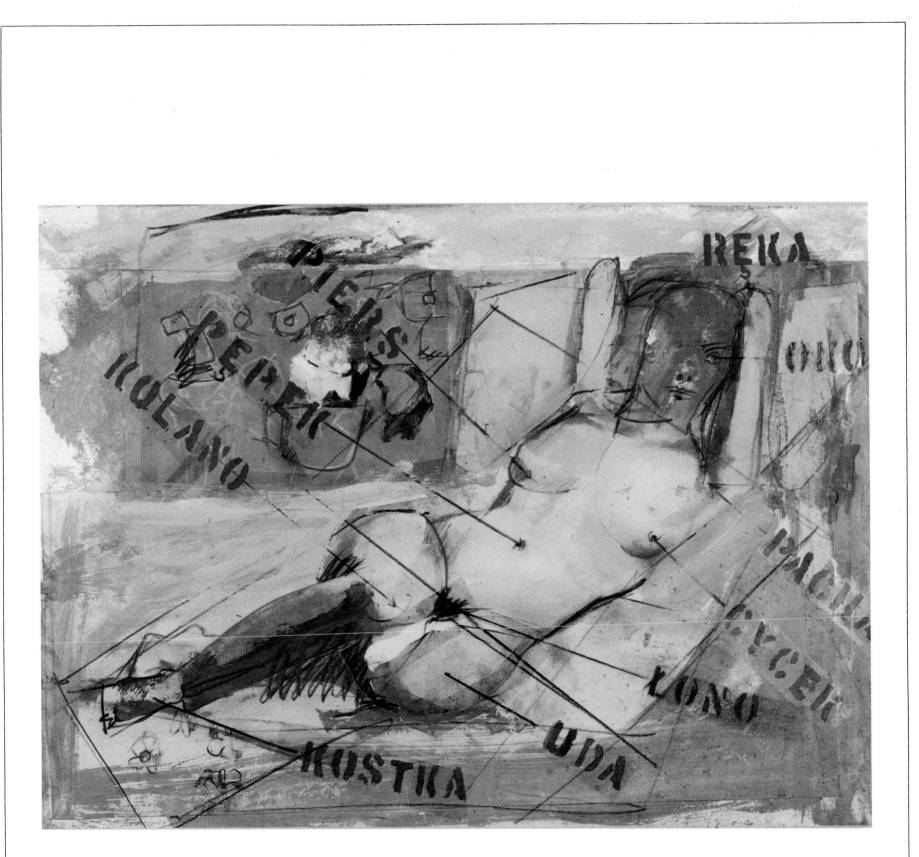

Parts of the Body—Polish, c.1962

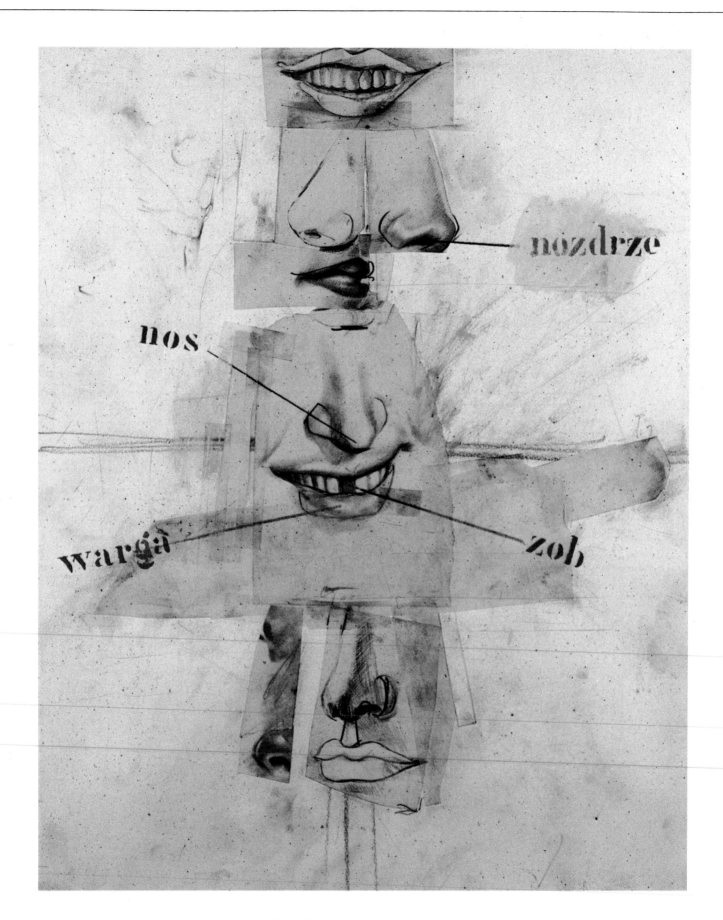

Polish Vocabulary Lesson, 1962

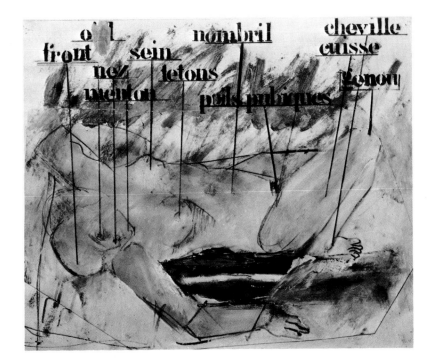

Parts of the Body: Sienna Figure, 1962

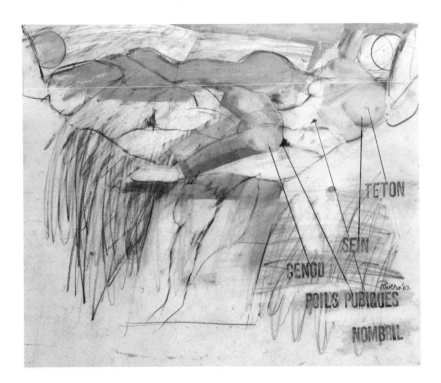

Visage, 1963

Portrait of Manoucher Yektai, 1961–2

How to Draw: Reclining Nudes and Rectangles with Legs, 1962

Parts of the Body: Italian Vocabulary Lesson, c. 1963

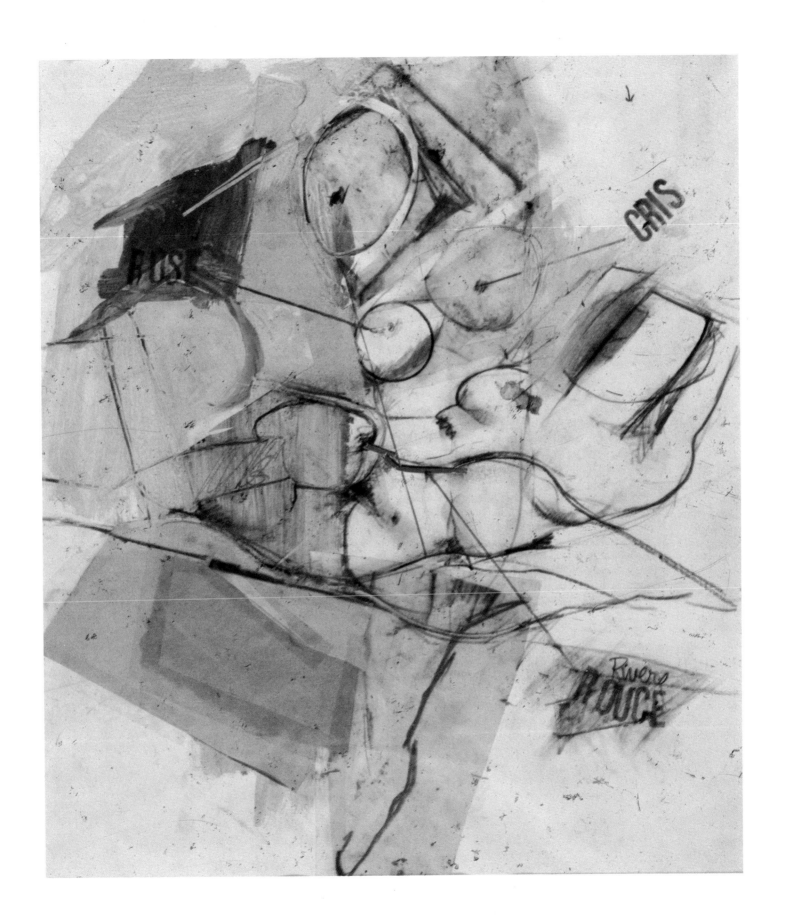

149

Actual 100-franc note

Bank Note, 1962

I did so many French moneys that they keep showing up all over the place.

I like them. I always liked this series. Somehow I think it harks back to my second visit to France, a certain period when I did a lot of paintings I liked. I did *Vocabulary Lessons* there and I did *French Money* and I did *Cigarettes*. I was able to repeat these subjects without getting tired of them. I look back on them as great years.

Double French Money, 1962

French Money III, 1962

Discontinued French Money, 1976

This is from a final orgy on French money. I think I must have done about fifteen of them.

Six French Money, 1962

Rivers at Gimpel, announcement for show at Gimpel Fils in London, 1964

SEVEN

ENGLAND, FRANCE, AND FRIENDS

The early sixties. This was the time when the reputation of American painters had become important in Europe in a way that had never happened before. We were invited to exhibitions all over the place. The scene was very important: collectors, museum people, painters, cocktail parties. There was the Venice Biennale in '62; some rich collector rented a ferry that took us to a distant island where there was the most sumptuous, insane meal with thousands of lobsters.

At about this time, Bill Brooker, an English guy and head of the Ealing School, read about me and decided I was going to make some kind of splash on the English scene. He invited me there to deliver a lecture, which is one of the ways you establish your position in the English art world. Collectors don't have the same power there, since there isn't that much money spent on contemporary art. The only way that a painter can know whether he is recognized by the world as having accomplished something is by the positions he gets at universities and art schools. And so unless I'm myth making now, I think that my being invited to speak at the Ealing School and the Victoria Albert Museum for the Royal College, constituted a kind of recognition on the part of the English. There wasn't any money involved.

Bill Brooker's invitation triggered a number of other invitations, and I spoke all over London and throughout England—Bristol, Bath. . . .

I was also there to marry Clarice and to meet her friends, but at the same time I was taking this chance to project myself on the English scene. And considering that I was a complete foreigner and there for the first time, things seemed to go very well. I was noticed immediately and felt at home and was invited to a lot of things. I think in those days I was much more egocentric, and the lectures were full of theatre.

I was taking a very tough attitude toward realism then; even though my works were very realistic, I said that really wasn't what they were about. I used the example of the yellow grapefruit—it was the yellowness and the roundness that interested me; that it was a grapefruit was not exactly important. Actually, I think quite differently now than I did in those days, and I think my statement was some kind of acquiescence to the popularity of abstract art in that period.

Bill Brooker, 1961

I liked what Bill Brooker looked like. He was kind of a round, very light-faced Englishman, proud of being a cockney. He was the English equivalent—with the kind of spirit—of someone like Jackson Pollock who wants to appear like an ordinary Joe, you know—just a drunk. I think that these English types who actually come from working-class backgrounds, they make no bones about it. They aren't interested in being thought upper-class Englishmen. Brooker was the first working-class sort I met who became someone in the art world.

I think that if one analyzes a lot of these drawings

from the early sixties one can see certain roots in some of the charcoal drawings by de Kooning which interested me at the time. A drawn line, an erasure, a tentative line drawn over it, some black and white splotches. . . . On the other hand, I think his sense of naturalism is different from mine. I don't think he was interested in muscle structure, bone structure, where the head was—something that looked like a head coming higher up on the page than something that looked like a leg. In these drawings of mine, and this one of Bill Brooker, I did try to get the look of one leg over the knee of the other.

I Like David Sylvester, 1962

Harry Matthews as a Football Player, 1962

Do you know the French writer Huysmans who wrote *Against the Grain*? I feel that Harry is that kind of writer who delights in imparting information; he's the last of those guys who know a good wine, where the best hotel in a particular small city is, what church is great on the way down to the south of France. I don't know the word for him—he's just someone who is full of good taste in all sorts of fields.

He's built like a football player, tall, big shoulders. And this drawing was done during a period in the sixties when I was simplifying and trying to make whatever got into the drawing into one big shape.

I did this drawing which is rather a spare version of Mary McCarthy in Paris in '62 in her apartment. I respected her as a big brain and a heavy intellectual. In those days I was completely enamored of anybody who could use Marxist language or who could talk about politics in a certain easy flowing way. I have a lot of ideas on politics, and I have this fantasy that someday I'd really like to be a political writer. And her reviews and articles were always exciting to me. The funny thing is that she said that doing those articles was like nothing for her. She had trouble with what she considered the creative stuff—her novels.

I met her, I did this drawing. She comes out rather tough-looking here, but she was quite kind to me. She was married to a man who was in the diplomatic corps and who knew a lot about Eastern Europe, and she got me visas to all those countries that were difficult to enter at that time. I haven't seen her in years. But whenever I see an article by her I'll read it. She was very smart, very helpful—also very funny.

Portrait of Mary McCarthy, 1962

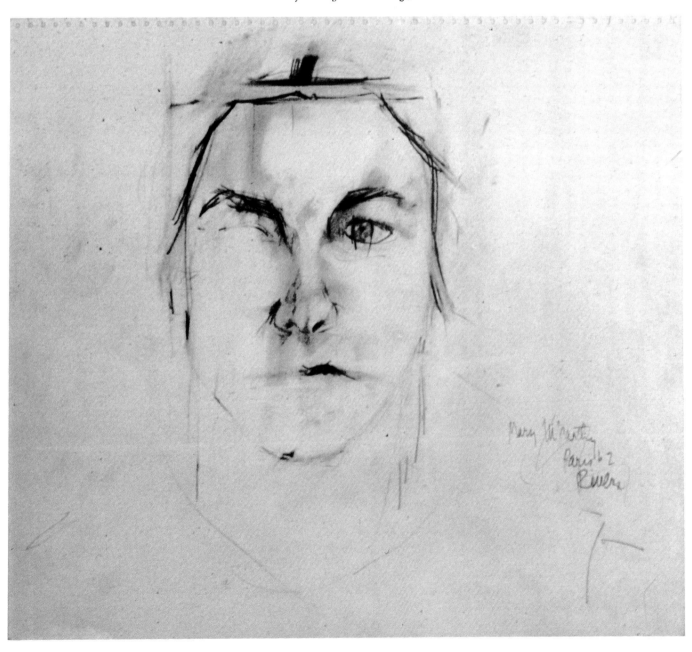

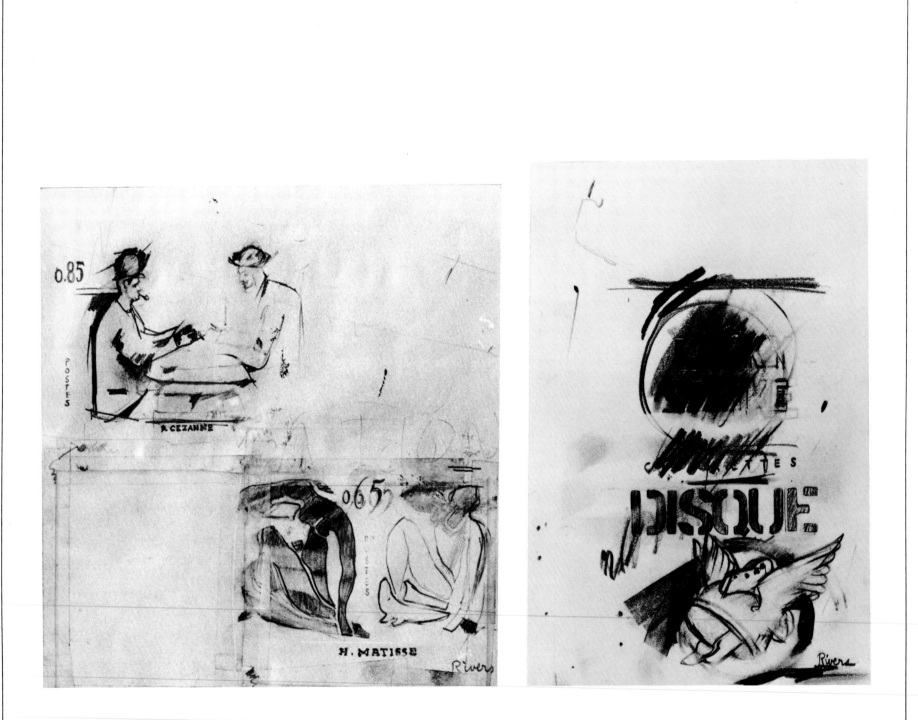

French Postage Stamps, 1963　　　　　*Friendship of America and France Drawing, 1961*

Pierre Restany was a French critic I met through Yves Klein, Jean Tinguely, and others when I was in Paris in the early sixties. He wrote about the *nouveau réalistes*. He came to the United States to lecture and I did this drawing during one of those visits. It was just after the period of all the "vocabulary lessons," so instead of going into eyes, nose, ears, I got bored and just did the moustache and labeled it *moustache*. Somewhere along the line I tore it up without realizing what I was doing and I had to piece it all back together.

Moustache, Portrait of Pierre Restany, 1962

161

Portrait of Lukas Foss, 1963

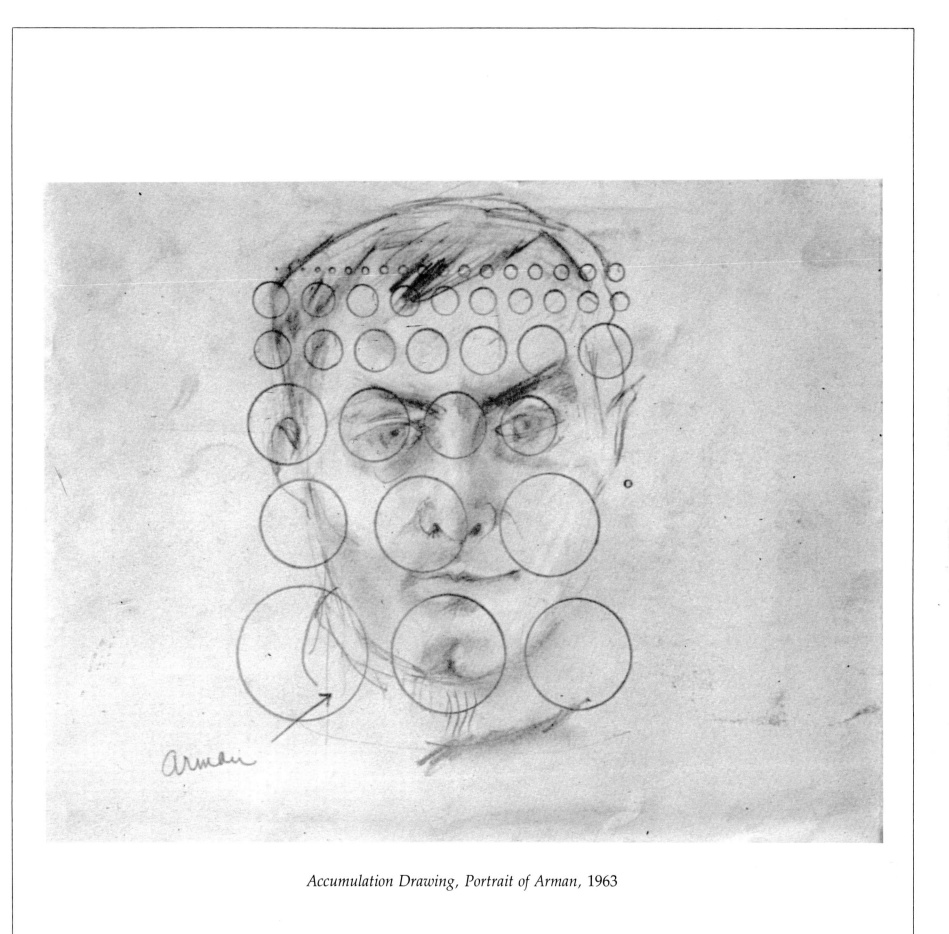

Accumulation Drawing, Portrait of Arman, 1963

Xerox Drawing of "Oil" McGrath, 1968

Portrait of Taylor, 1966

Terry Southern. My pal "Tex." When did I do this? Pretty late, early seventies. I've had a long friendship with Terry, I like his work, think he's funny; he's a mess, but he's also marvelous. He's a picture of the human condition. If there's a median where you're OK, and one side is heading toward being awful and the other toward possibly being beautiful and poetic, he's somewhere between the median and the bottom. He eats too much, he drinks too much; at the same time he's so funny and strangely polite and gentle. Public delicacy is very touching.

I did this drawing because I think that by now if I know a guy for a certain number of years, he begins to feel, well, how come you're not drawing me—you're drawing everybody else? So I think, let me see, did I draw that person?—as if I have to take care of this particular thing which is the relationship of artists to other artists. At the time that I did it I didn't think that I got a likeness at all; I just worked all afternoon and I gave up. Now that some time has passed, I think it looks just like him. I did it when we were working on *The Donkey and the Darling* in his home in Connecticut. It was a way of taking up some time. I would just do the face, and in a certain way I'm bothered now that I didn't do more full-figured people, but I seem to save that for my painting.

Tex, Portrait of Terry Southern, 1971

How to Draw Horses, 1961

Kiki, 1965-6

Camels, 1962

Camel Drawing, 1962

French Camel Carbon Paper, 1976

"I hate the idea of the 'serious' artist. I'm against the Albert Schweitzer story, the Judy Garland story, and Pablo Casals; what an object of cultural flag waving he's become.

Fragment, *Head of Frank O'Hara*, 1954

FRANK O'HARA

EULOGY FOR FRANK O'HARA

Frank was my best friend. I always thought he would be the first to die among my small happy group. But I daydreamed a romantic death brought about by too much whiskey, by smoking three packs of Camels a day, by too much sex, by unhappy love affairs, by writing too many emotional poems, too many music and dance concerts, just too much living which would drain away his energy and his will to live. His death was on my mind all the sixteen years I knew him and I told him this. I was worried about him because he loved me. His real death is a shock because he died—and died horribly in an absurd situation.

Frank was killed on the soft, safe, white sand of Long Island. This extraordinary man lay without a pillow in a bed that looked like a large crib. He was purple wherever his skin showed through the white hospital gown. He was a quarter larger than usual. Every few inches there was some sewing composed of dark blue thread. Some stitching was straight and

three or four inches long, others were longer and semicircular. The lids of both eyes were bluish black. It was hard to see his beautiful blue eyes which receded a little into his head. He breathed with quick gasps. His whole body quivered. There was a tube in one of his nostrils down to his stomach. On paper, he was improving. In the crib he looked like a shaped wound, an innocent victim of someone else's war. His leg bone was broken and splintered and pierced his skin. Every rib was cracked. A third of his liver was wiped out by the impact. What can talking about it do. I don't know.

Frank O'Hara was my best friend. There are at least sixty people in New York who thought Frank O'Hara was their best friend. Without a doubt he was the most impossible man I knew. He never let me off the hook. He never allowed me to be lazy. His talk, his interests, his poetry, his life was a theatre in which I saw what human beings are *really* like. He was a dream of contradictions. At one time or another, he was everyone's greatest and most loyal audience. His friendships were so strong he forced me to reassess men and women I would normally not have bothered to know. He was a professional handholder. His fee was love. It is easy to deify in the presence of death but Frank *was* an extraordinary man—everyone here knows it.

For me, Frank's death is the beginning of tragedy. My first experience with loss.

Springs, Long Island   *July 27, 1966*

O'Hara Reading, 1967

Here he is after he died—up in heaven reading and being watched by Allen Ginsberg and LeRoi Jones. It comes from an actual reading at the Living Theatre, I believe, in the early sixties. Someone took photographs and I worked from them. In fact, this print is partially photographic.

oh oh god how I'd love to dream let alone sleep it's night
the soft air wraps me like a swarm it's raining and I have
a cold I am a real human being with real ascendancies
and a certain amount of rapture what do you do with a kid
like me if you don't eat me I'll have to eat myself

it's a strange curse my "generation" has we're all
like the flowers in the Agassiz Museum perpetually ardent
don't touch me because when I tremble it makes a noise
like a Chinese wind-bell it's that I'm seismographic is all
and when a Jesuit has stared you down for ever after you clink

I wonder if I've really scrutinized this experience like
you're supposed to have if you can type there's not much
soup left on my sleeve energy creativity guts ponderableness
lent is coming in imponderableness "I'd like to die smiling" ugh
and a very small tiptoe is crossing the threshold away

whither Lumumba whither oh whither Gauguin
I have often tried to say goodbye to strange fantoms I
read about in the newspapers and have always succeeded
though the ones at "home" are dependent on Dependable
Laboratory and Sales Company on Pulaski Street strange

I think it's goodbye to a lot of things like Christmas
and the Mediterranean and halos and meteorites and villages
full of damned children well it's goodbye then as in Strauss
or some other desperately theatrical venture it's goodbye
to lunch to love to evil things and to the ultimate good as "well"

the strange career of a personality begins at five and ends
forty minutes later in a fog the rest is just a lot of stranded
ships honking their horns full of joy-seeking cadets in bloomers
and beards it's okay with me but must they cheer while they honk
it seems that breath could easily fill a balloon and drift away

scaring the locusts in the straggling grey of living dumb
exertions then the useful noise would come of doom of data
turned to elegant decoration like a strangling prince once ordered
no there is no precedent of history no history nobody came before
nobody will ever come before and nobody ever was that man

you will not die not knowing this is true this year

Illustration for poem "For the Chinese New Year and for Bill
Berkson" by Frank O'Hara from *In Memory of My Feelings*, 1969

In Memory of the Dead, 1967

This is my morbid self, 1967. I call it *Memory of the Dead*. Frank had been dead about a year, and my mother-in-law for about ten years. I just juxtaposed them both.

This piece is a memorial to our collaboration. It seems as though now Frank O'Hara has become some kind of culture figure, having died at the age that he did. His reputation far exceeds how he was regarded when he was alive—which is sort of interesting.

He's a tragic figure. He died in a very terrible way. He was a very interesting, attractive person. He had a tremendous amount of affection for a lot of people, and when he was drunk a lot of aggression, and the difference between when he was drunk and when he was sober was so arresting. But he had such a lively mind he was always sort of exciting to be with. He was also just a good dopey friend—you didn't have to do a frigging thing.

The last time he came by was once in June of 1966. He said, "Want a blow job?"—it was a joke between us—and I said, "Come on in, why not?" I mean the things that go on between people are sometimes so insane. And by the time we got through, I don't know—it just wasn't bad. And three weeks later he died. He was dead. And I often think about it—it'll be buried with me. I imagine it's what has gone on since the beginning of time. Like you're close to someone, you do something with them, and then they die fairly shortly after that particular thing, and it gives what you've done another twist. I've heard people say things like, "The day before he died he saw his mother," and it's as if the guy died in peace—the death became something else because something happened. So I've often thought of this. I was very glad that I did that. I don't know why. What's the difference? It's buried with him. One more experience—what does it do to the body that's lying in the grave?

At least I didn't say no. And look—what I mean is, what are we regretting?

In this one I juxtaposed a lot of different things from my studio and sort of made up a little story about me—my childhood, my mother. I mean, it's like writing a short story in collage, so to speak. It doesn't make any sense, but on the basis of the raw material you have around, with the collage you can actually

Don't Fall and Me, 1966

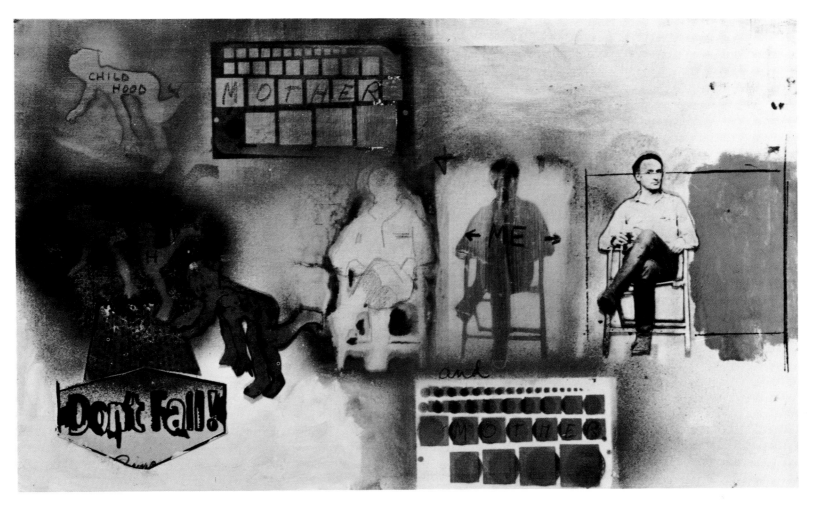

work out something. This one consists of really separate works, like *The Elimination of Nostalgia*, for example. I used the photograph, a small version, and I traced it. Then I brought in my mother behind this template. . . . It's a chutzpah number, really. I like the division of it, and where things are; it's a pleasant work. But I think

that to endow it with any more meaning—it's just one of those misleading works that seem pregnant with meaning, but don't add up. And the next thing you know someone comes along and agrees with something you never even meant, and it's gone. Someone buys it.

In the old days I remember thinking to myself that even the worst reasons can produce some good and interesting results. A person may sit down and say he's going to write a poem because he wants to bug someone, and his motives may be completely unrelated to what finally appears. I did a painting called *The Elimination of Nostalgia*, as if doing the most nostalgic thing would get rid of it. It was a portrait of myself in leather boots, a very macho family man, my sons and my wife in a Victorian pose from a photograph. The title, *Elimination . . .*, was to show that I had no interest in it. But actually it couldn't help but be nostalgic, and it is. As you're working, you really don't know what the end result of these things is going to be.

Maybe what I was doing was what anthropologists call exorcising the spirits. I don't know. But it's always on my mind, I constantly think about it because I've been accused of nostalgia. And nostalgia—at least in the forties and fifties—was always deprecated. A high-brow type or an intellectual was supposed to separate himself from a folk interest. You were supposed to be ashamed of it. So it's been a conflict. . . . It's like the problem with the superego. I mean, the "parents" say it's no good, but you're attracted to it and at the same time you think maybe they're right. When I see it on TV, or when I see the general

culture's interest in nostalgia today it does repel me. It's like instant affection; if somebody mentions an old song you're supposed to go "Oh God, isn't that beautiful."

While the artist or the poet may deal with nostalgia, or memories, or soft things of the past, I think it is incumbent upon him to present these things in some harder or clearer or more detailed light, because under that glare I think you'll see it another way. What starts out as nostalgia becomes something else. . . . There are so many things that come into your mind when you start. How do you want to come off? What part does your work play in projecting you in the world as some kind of personality, as some kind of spirit? And you might think that your work should be devoid of that. You should just somehow like something about the color or something about the face or the pose. But there are other considerations and maybe that's what makes it worth doing, because you never can really decide what is leading you on, what are aesthetic considerations and what are ego concerns and commodity concerns. What is leading your hand? And the more you are aware of the dualities, ambiguities, contradictions in your character, the richer your work is, really. Only naïve people think that what they do is pure and beautiful and full of . . . the *right* thing.

Elimination of Nostalgia I, 1967

Portrait of Henry Geldzahler, 1964

ART AND THE SIXTIES

I'm afraid that Henry Geldzahler looks a little piggy in this drawing. At that time he didn't have a beard, and he had enough hair to kind of cover most of the parts where there wasn't hair. Then I think he finally gave up—that's my own fantasy of what this man was doing. On the other hand, he looks substantial and serious and Monet-ish.

He's always been an interesting person around New York. This is one of the drawings that appears in *The Golden Oldies.* It may have been name dropping on my part to include the former head of the Met. At the time he was just a young man that I knew. He's very smart, he's powerful, he's worrisome. He left me out of an exhibition that was very important once, which I think was rather devastating since it was "painter's of the sixties" or something like that. I couldn't completely comprehend why. He didn't have to be crazy about my work, but I had made enough of a splash—I don't know why he did that. I think that he was still living out his fantasy of pleasing the critic Clem

Greenberg, or maybe he actually felt that somehow I didn't come up to snuff. I couldn't be sure.

I have a very tough time with establishment acceptance, strangely enough. My work is known. I'm not a poor starving artist, I admit that. I'm in a lot of museums, a lot of collections in Europe and America. But there's some aspect of the establishment, and by that I mean those whose tastes count for certain things in the art community—mostly critics and directors who have identified themselves with contemporary art—who find that there's something about the way I perceive things which either seems to make fun of art or at times just gets to be, maybe too much. And so I've had trouble. . . . I've never had a show of any of my work in the Guggenheim even when Lawrence Alloway made an exhibition of contemporary drawings.

You ask if there's a connection between the sort of criticism that comes from certain establishment quarters and my style as a visual diarist, and, you know, I think perhaps there is. I look back now and I see that it's true that I'm more of a storyteller than I thought I was. And there was a great animosity against "literary" painting for a long time.

I grew up in an era in which revolutionary or radical ideas were being tried in every aspect of cultural life—writing, art, politics. I think that my work could be thought very progressive, but it also could seem to be harkening back to an earlier period and ignoring all the "advances." You had people like Clem Greenberg or even Harold Rosenberg—although he was a more liberal, human type—who kept their eyes on certain aspects of the art world. Where did you stand in the political spectrum? Were you fighting a conservative battle or were you fighting a radical battle? Where did you seem to throw your weight? And I think that very early on they assumed that either I was undefinable, or seemed to be throwing my weight in a retrogressive, conservative direction. In fact, it took me a long time to accept my concern with subject matter. I tried to hide it in some way and include other things in my earlier work which I think was quite natural, given the pressures and the kind of attention abstract expressionism got. I think that I fared pretty well. I didn't capitulate completely like so many people who are one kind of painter one day and the next day they're another kind of painter. I held on to some thread.

But I don't know. When I think about the painter Richard Lindner and that steadiness of spirit, I wonder about my own. He was an example of one of these people who stuck. We're all stuck in what we do. But if no one pays attention it seems harder to continue doing what you're "stuck" with. Lindner had friends in the art world who admired him—so he wasn't a total failure. But for a very, very long time the things that we recognize as "recognition" were not coming toward him. Critics didn't pay attention. Magazines didn't have articles about him. Maybe his shows were reviewed, but very infrequently. One slowly became aware of Lindner's work. And finally, of course, whenever you're confronted with a man who was ignored throughout and stuck to his guns, and then is recognized, admired, and suddenly becomes a household word, you begin to think about your own character, about your own way in art. Just how did I proceed? What has my life in art been about?

When he died I went to see the show and then I spoke to the widow and I was asked by *Art in America* to do an obituary about him. I thought quite a bit about him and somewhere along the line I began to wonder if I waivered in my own resolve about things. I think that I got recognition in some way; maybe there's no artist alive who feels he's gotten "proper" recognition—but I think people knew about me, people liked me, people didn't like me. But what was I about? How much does the public really know about me? What about me has been filtered by the very way that I present myself? After all, everybody makes up their own myth, their own story.

I think there was a point, for instance, in the late fifties or early sixties when the whole thing of abstract painting was *so strong*, so recognized and so thought about, so on everybody's mind, every museum director who was worth his weight had to think up something—and it was big business. Careers were based on it. And there I was off in some corner by myself—but attracted to it, like anybody else would be. It was shiny, it was glitter, right? And it was not only glitter, it was gold. I wondered—at what point did I lose a certain kind of confidence in what I was doing, and move slowly toward doing that other thing. . . . Is that what art is about? Is that maybe what life and art is about?

I think what happened with Lindner was that he already was so much what he was, he couldn't change. He was older, he was over twenty years older than I was. By the time he came to America none of this business had started yet. It took place later, and his character and his work had been established if not for the public, at least for himself. To have changed would have been such an assassination of character, although other artists did it. But he was a cynical man, he was a tough guy in certain ways, he was maybe even a defeated man. . . . So I read him in many ways—probably just reading myself, because I didn't know him that well. I knew him . . . as you say . . . as a "colleague."

We both did the same thing, there was some kind of relationship between our spirits. I appreciated the rhetoric he built up around his work. He invented the whole world of Bertolt Brecht—he painted the funny people, he had this whole thing about pimps, criminals, and certain kinds of women. He saw—or he was able to make up—some kind of relationship between all that talk and his work. I feel that we had something in common because of our continued interest in realism, and that at least we thought there was a relationship between what we painted and what we say or think about the world. When I'm talking about *Napoleon*, when I'm talking about *French Money*, I am talking about things I perceive in the world. There's a certain semantic relationship: I paint, and then I can talk about my work in a way that deals with the world. Lindner was closer to having a world view. "Artists are really criminals," he would say, and he would immediately get someone to say, "What do you mean?" And then he would have a whole idea about that. Now how did that get into his work? I don't know, but he could talk about the world and relate it to his work.

This is a very different approach from the approach of an abstract expressionist. He tells you about brown or blue. In other words, the experience is there on the canvas. It doesn't relate to anything else. It's fresh, it's new, it breaks your bonds from the world; it makes you aware of life, certain qualities like musical qualities. You're a Mozart—you're not thinking of woods, forests, lions, are you? You are just thrilling to some sound—some sound and some kind of intelligence. Well, that's what I think abstract painting is about. Color and some kind of organization which is interesting to you.

When I look back I can remember how I was influenced by that. You read about a sale or about how well someone is doing, or you hear that Jackson Pollock is being given a show or that this is happening to Mark Rothko. I knew these people. These were people who were living people in my life. I knew that they were older than me—not that much older, you understand, but old enough for me not to be congenitally jealous. It didn't absorb me day and night and really hurt me the way it does when somebody exactly your own age, gets that kind of attention. With a guy like Pollock or Rothko I could say, well, they're older—it should come to them first. But at the same time I just kept thinking, "God, I mean everybody is thinking about that work," and I felt left out somewhere in a corner.

I guess one of the points when I felt it most poignantly was when I was working on *Washington Crossing the Delaware*, which is '53. But all along, right through the fifties, I felt it. Yet I'm such a funny person—I had almost the opposite feeling too, which is that there *was* some relationship between my work and theirs. In other words, I *wasn't* that much off in a corner. *Other* people thought I was off in a corner, critics like Greenberg, who were defining what the avant-garde was. But actually it worked out OK. Because they were "that," then suddenly I was "this." If I wasn't the most popular thing, at least I was this "it." Miraculously, I seemed to draw some attention.

But these kind of concerns—you remember them, and suddenly ten, fifteen years go by, and they seem like hallucination, smoke. Now I'm wondering if what I was really up to was off in some other place, because I'm beginning to realize now that other things speak to people—not this or that genre but some force in your work that comes across.

So you never really know all the things you may be doing at a particular moment. Other people have to recognize something. An artist comes along like Reinhardt and does black paintings, and he says, "What's the use of all these kinds of frills with reds and greens and things like that—I'll do black painting." And a man stands in front of it and has the same idea. He says, "What's the use of all the greens, reds, blues. . . ." Then another guy could say, "I see a void, a dark urn in which I can place my own thoughts." What I'm trying to say is there's such a wide spectrum that whoever is looking at it or whoever is interested can see many things. All these artists in the fifties and sixties can't believe what they sounded like—how a work of art had to be understood in the way *they* understood it.

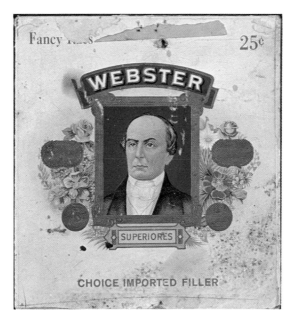

Actual Webster cigar-box label

Carbon Webster, 1962

Webster and Europe, 1967

Take this drawing of Howard Kanovitz. Cigar in hand. This is what Hollywood would call a guy thinking hard. Now, what are we looking at? Are we looking at Howard Kanovitz and the kind of psychologically singular individual that comes to be Howard Kanovitz under my pencil? Or are we looking at the width of the face, the amount of detail, the shadow of the nose which turns out to be sort of a dribble right down the left side? What is it about? And so you're caught. It's an age-old drama. It's content, it's style. You can say these two dimensions coexist, but why did Ad Reinhardt feel that there is no content apart from what appears on the paper? I know that this question about form vs. content, or realism vs. the plastic, abstract qualities, comes up for me a great deal. I swing in and out. Is that the dilemma of trying to be modern?

Anyway, this is a drawing of Howard Kanovitz, who is an artist, and a very good artist—who has this weird thing of being fantastically famous in Germany. An American Jew from Fall River, Massachusetts, ends up being America's number one painter in Germany. He's an airbrush realist. A very good painter, very thorough—something I thought he'd never become. He painted abstractly when he was younger.

We have been friends for many, many years, and we have the same kind of background. We're both Jews and we come from parents who didn't speak "too good English." He played a musical instrument first. He came to New York as a jazz musician trying to be an artist. We were both that: jazz musician, artist. He took my loft in New York when I moved out to the country and "gave up New York" because of love. And we've been friends, you know, all the time. Next to Frank and a guy called Earl McGrath and just a handful of other people, he is my oldest friend. We continue to see each other through all the changes in our work and in life. He's been very helpful. There was a period in which I was heavy into airbrush, and he gave me many, many hints and help. He's technically more adept than I am, and yet—you know what takes place when old friends do the same thing— there's that competitive undertone. But somehow you manage to deal with it, and we have dealt with it.

Portrait of Howard Kanovitz, 1964

John Gruen in Plastic, c. 1966

Lions from the Dreyfus Fund, 1969

Portrait of a Budding Art Historian, 1968

This is a portrait of an art historian who is seated in front of a Piranesi, an eighteenth-century architectural draftsman. It's a collage and I cut her out and put her in front of it as some kind of comment on her interests. . . . This was done toward the end of my interest in Day-Glo color, when I was using it less and less until it finally got to be little strips. Actually, it still does something to what would have otherwise been an ordinary picture. Cover the strip and you'll see the difference. The Day-Glo puts it on another level. It's very jarring.

The girl was a student who was doing a term paper on me. She came down from Boston to see me and we became close. Later she began going out with Bill Rubin, who was the head of the Museum of Modern Art. I found out from her that he couldn't understand how he could possibly be going with a girl who at one time was interested in me. Like a lot of people who didn't know me and only heard rumors, he had a very distorted notion of who I was. Since he had problems with my work, he dismissed me as an individual as well.

No Name Portrait, 1968

"I still remember that when I was in public school there was a guy in front of me, Ralph Robinson, who used to draw horses (maybe he's still alive). I would be peeking over his shoulder—I couldn't believe what this guy did, he was so marvelous. The best I could do was draw maps. . . . Actually, I was always surprised that people said that I was such a good draftsman. I always feel when I start to draw that I don't know if I'm going to get it, truthfully speaking. Maybe it's just that idea that maybe I *won't* get it that attracts me."

—*Dick Cavett Interview*

This is a portrait of Lenin. I had just read Isaac Deutscher's trilogy on the life of Trotsky and I was interested in doing something on the Russian Revolution. Lenin in particular had begun to emerge as a figure for me.

It's a cut-up photo, a collage. That tie was actually a piece of cloth stapled on to the work. I began feeling strongly about these materials, like that pink paper I used which had large grooves like a record; from top to bottom I wanted the portrait to gain something from the physical qualities of that paper. Later I did a print of this, no longer three dimensional of course. . . .

When I went to the Soviet Union in 1976 I showed slides of this and *The History of The Russian Revolution*. It was like bringing coals to Newcastle. In the American Embassy there was a very pretty Russian woman—obviously a suspect person. I mean, can a Russian work in an American Embassy without being used by the Russians? But when I left I gave her a print of the *Lenin* and a kiss. Later, after I had come back for a bag I forgot, she was sitting at her desk looking at the picture in the most insane way. What is this artist trying to say? Why did he do Lenin? What does Lenin mean to an American?

Lenin with Tie, 1965

Rembrandt, *Syndics of the Drapers' Guild*, 1662

Actual Dutch Masters cigar-box label

One night in the early sixties I passed something on the Long Island Expressway just before the Queens tunnel that I must have seen for years, the billboard advertising cigars, Dutch Masters. I suddenly realized it was sort of perfect. It's weird, isn't it? You're looking at Rembrandt—in neon! Advertising cigars. It was too much, it was irresistible!

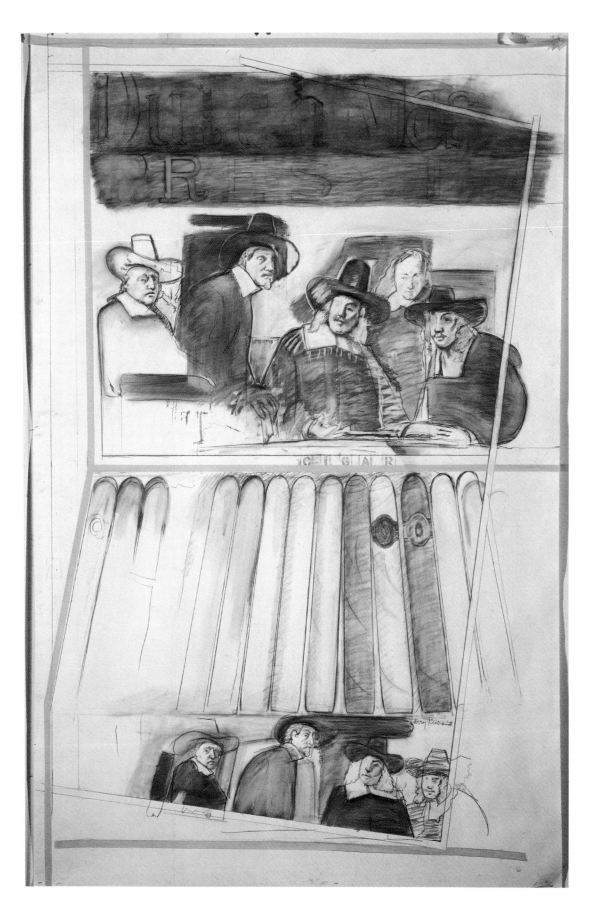

Golden Oldies: Dutch Masters, 1978

Mauve Masters, 1963

Dutch Masters VF, c. 1963

Dutch Masters Silver, 1968

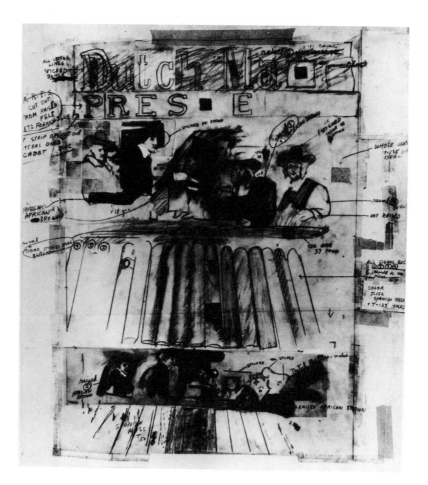

Dutch Masters, drawing for banner, c.1966

Silver Infanta, 1968

MULTIMEDIA

I took a fair amount of drugs in the sixties. This is a personal thing; its so difficult to deal with; drugs are usually so destructive that to talk about the part that is constructive may be dangerous—some poor individual may pick up the book somewhere and read it and get the wrong idea. . . . But at any rate the truth of the matter is that I used to get so despondent about things and unable to deal with things—when I took drugs, for a few days at least I didn't care what was happening. The responsibilities that were usually felt to be mine were suddenly abandoned. But I didn't work under the influence of drugs. I didn't work "high." I couldn't. If I smoked pot, it would be social. If I took heroin, I would lie down. I never had a heroin habit, but I did take it from time to time.

Heroin gives you a rush where you go from sitting there feeling very normal—like your eyes hurt, your asshole hurts, you're feeling a little hungry—and suddenly you become one warm, wonderful unit, interested in very little except just lying around touching someone maybe, and talking in very nice soft tones. And so you didn't work—those aren't working conditions. Any idea I have to do with making art can only be expressed in a very sober, aggressive mood.

Actually, you can't believe the primitive conditions under which I would take heroin—the dirt! When I was going to Hans Hofmann's some guys came to see me to shoot up; I would stop drawing and go into the bathroom. Once we found the top of an ink bottle, we cleaned it out and started to cook up the stuff, and some of the ink came out in the heroin. We weren't going to waste it—we drew it up into the needle, I shot it into my arm and nothing ever happened.

After I took it I'd go home and go to sleep and feel pretty terrible the next day. A day after that I'd be all right and I'd start to work, and then I wouldn't see anybody again for ten days. And then some guy would come around and maybe we'd do it for two days. I would always say, Oh, get lost. I would sort of put these guys down. I didn't like the kind of people they were. They were like those monosyllabic, everything-is-understood, you-don't-talk-about-anything kind of people that I really despise. They still exist.

I'm a classic type. I do things and I hate what I do. It's very old-fashioned, really, like the person who walks down the street and picks up what he thinks is low-life, takes her back to the room, and fucks—and then feels very dirty for a few days. I think I felt that way about drugs. It's connected with sorrow and self-pity, and a certain pleasure that it gives you in the body. There was a time when I did it much more often—when I was a musician in the forties and on the road. But I didn't do it that often. I knew enough about it. I stopped about ten years ago. A bad batch nearly killed me; something happened, I just changed.

In the middle sixties I started taking speed, which a friend of mine (who exaggerated my interest in heroin). He took me to a doctor who gave vitamin shots, but along with those vitamins was amphetamine. For a month I used to go up to get the shots, but finally I just got the ampules and took the dose myself. With speed I didn't get what you call a "rush." I never shot it mainline and that was probably the reason. There was something about putting a fast drug, an "up" drug into your vein that scared me. But it did give me energy. I guess it just makes the heart beat faster, but whatever it is it didn't seem to make me feel that different. Actually people tell me that I *was* different, that I was boring, that I talked a lot. People complained about my personality, and I think that at that

It was on speed that I did a lot of the three-dimensional works using new materials and carpentry. As I look back on them now, I have the same feeling that I have about the work of other periods when I didn't take speed—which is that some I like, and some I don't. It isn't that I thought they were great when I did them and I look back now and see them as lousy. I went through all sorts of things as I was doing them, just as I did during any other time: I start out with great enthusiasm, begin to do it, find that I don't like it so much, get desperate, try to work very hard, work it out and finally accept what I've done. It's a process that's been with me my whole life.

In the seventies I started to do coke, which I never did when I was younger, but somehow I didn't like it. Coke didn't come out of my music background. It came more from my own uptown social milieu. I cut that out because I felt that it began to affect my health. I thought actually that maybe it did something to my hearing.

There's a deeper question about drugs: why do you take drugs and what part of taking drugs has to do

time people began to mistrust me as an artist. They see that you're talking a mile a minute and you're not very conscious of what other people are going through; you sound like a blowhard, so maybe what you do isn't that worthwhile.

Prior to the sixties taking drugs in the art field was considered pretty odd. (Now if you don't take drugs you're almost not considered an artist.) I was probably one of the first ones in the milieu that I worked in who took drugs—and so I think that I was mistrusted for a long while because of it. If I have any theories about art establishment reactions to me, I think it has something to do with all of this. A guy staggering around a bar is OK. I mean Pollock could be a drunk and still work; that was something people were familiar with—it just shows you how primitive those attitudes are.

But I did work under speed. It kept me up—probably at a little higher level, and I know now what speed does, why it is called speed. I probably am suffering all the physical problems that I am suffering these days because of those three years in which I did speed every day.

with the idea of "boredom" and being an artist? Now to answer that question is very hard. What do I mean by "boredom" and why am I bored? Is taking drugs the same thing as doing art—to alleviate your boredom? I don't know. They're two forms: one the world accepts because it seems to have some constructive value—you give something to society. And with the other you're just putting some stuff in your veins and you're not giving anything. When I say there have been more alterations to the face of painting because of the artist's boredom, I don't think I'm referring to the kind of boredom you have that leads you to take drugs. Drugs have more to do with avoiding a certain kind of pain. I think that the constructive value of drugs for me was that they enabled me to hit the bottom and to feel as if there was nothing else to really worry about or do. You couldn't straighten out anything, you couldn't make anything better; you may as well just paint and work.

For me the world seems to be that way now without drugs. There are days when I can turn off the phone and not do anything except work because it doesn't seem as though it's worth it. I mean the talking, the questions, the concerns, the ambition, the problems, the children, your wife, whatever, girl friends and all that. What's the difference? Forget it. And you work. I feel I'm building up for it now. You can tell the mood I'm in. I don't feel very good and I'm getting to care less and less about things. And I'll care less. And then I work.

I remember when I first did welding, spray cans, airbrush, plastic materials—there was always the ele-

ment of a toy, a new toy. And these new toys were always fresh and interesting. I also think that I probably carry that out in my life, which is rather disturbing. I mean I think that I have that feeling with people, with bodies. At the same time I could make a case for the opposite—that in my work at any rate there is some overall view or approach to subject matter that is there all the time. It's hard to know whether to give yourself a tinselly atmosphere or to present yourself as some old master with all the perennial values.

Putting an Eye on It, 1969

Anemones, 1963

Jim Dine Storm Window Portrait (position I), 1965

Jim Dine Storm Window Portrait (position II), 1965

Jim Dine Storm Window Portrait (position III), 1965

In all truthfulness this is the only work I ever dreamed. I was returning from Europe on a boat and I fell asleep in the middle of the afternoon, probably after drinking some wine at lunch, and I dreamed of Jim Dine in a storm window.

Jim Dine is a painter, a *great American painter*, and someone who is a friend of mine. The pleasure of this window is that it opens and shuts, and you can get three views.

This is foil and collage on a board with storm window. But there's drawing in it, too; it's a three-dimensional piece and the actual details were done on paper and glued on to Plexiglas. In the first position you have one version of a portrait, and then when you open the window you see different things behind. This is a collaboration with Niki de Saint-Phalle, Tinguely's wife, who decorated the piece.

Tinguely and I have an ongoing relationship. But in the sixties, of course, we saw each other much more. I used to go to Europe and he'd come here. He lived out in the country with me in 1966, and I guess that's when I did this. He worked, we all worked. At that point, he was really an international figure. Art and happenings: Jean Tinguely was a continuation of that movement. You remember the guys who became "earth artists"? In the early sixties Tinguely went out into the middle of the desert in Utah to work and he did one of those explosions—I'm not sure exactly what it was. In the middle sixties people began writing rather detrimentally about his exhibitions in the United States, and he just withdrew from the American scene. He got very upset with America. He felt Europe was his terrain where he was understood. He's probably the most well-known and liked artist in Europe.

We got along very well and we had a certain kind of rapport probably because we didn't understand each other very well. He didn't understand English too well and I didn't understand French too well; our relationship was in English—but very limited. I have a feeling he's much more intellectual than he sounds.

Tinguely is a Swiss, German-speaking guy who was in the Swiss army, who passes as a Frenchman because he speaks French and has a great reputation in Paris. He was a guy who was on skis during the war. He comes from farming, mountain people, and speaks about them in a very funny way. People have told me he's a good businessman, but I think this is a kind of prejudice people have against the Swiss. They think Swiss is banking.

Tinguely developed late. I don't think he started until he was in his early thirties, and before that he led a rather strange and interesting life. He hung around bars. He'd do little deals. He'd made a living that way. He had a real taste for a certain kind of life. He has a very peculiar identity—he walks around in laborer's clothes and he doesn't want to know rich people or collectors. At the same time he knew Pompidou. He's the most energetic, most dedicated worker that any of us know.

He has an interest in scale that is just sort of exciting. He makes things the size of this studio which is vast. He makes huge, heavy things moving; when I think of art—it's still, it doesn't move, it doesn't make a sound. And he comes along and sort of breaks this whole idea. He's sticking his thumb out at a lot of things, and I admire him for it.

Tinguely Storm Window Portrait (in collaboration with Niki de Saint Phalle), 1965

Miss Popcorn, 1972

Here is a one-time girl friend I did a lot of video with, Diana, *Miss Popcorn*. I guess maybe she was eighteen when I did this. There's a kind of cool, slick quality to the work—different from the others, maybe because it's airbrush on vinyl. I learned later that somehow it didn't seem to fit into a certain notion people have about my work—or that I have myself. It changed something in my art. It "neatened me up." The history or stages of the work were no longer part of it—I mean, how the work developed, my fingerprints and all that, went out of it. I use airbrush in a very different way today, more at the beginning of the work with stencils as an aid to placement for me so I know where things are, what size they are. And then I begin working with charcoal and a brush.

Reclining Models and Shoes, 1966

This is a former baby-sitter, who I will admit I tried to seduce, but it didn't work. A little Irish girl whose father was a telephone repairman. She was quite beautiful—I thought that hat looked marvelous and should be made three-dimensional. The kids liked her and I saw her grow up—she once came to me and told me that she smoked pot.

Actually, it's funny—knowing and being desirous of girls when they're teen-agers, and then you see them when they're twenty-one, and suddenly, they seem old. It sounds like chutzpah on my part—I mean, I'm getting there—but they not only seem old, they don't seem attractive. If you met them when they were twenty-one, they'd be young. Very odd.

Going with young girls can be absurd. Not so long ago I was standing in front of the Cedar with a girl friend and some old woman was making gestures to me which have to do with do I remember the time she and I were together? And I'm looking at this woman— this elderly woman—and it dawns on me: of course, she is a contemporary of mine. And the girl I'm with is looking at her in a certain way; by what magic am I escaping the effects of time. An interesting moment . and I remember back to when we *had* gone to bed, this woman and I, and I think that there was something about it that wasn't very satisfying for her. There was something about my attitude or something that was not so nice. And she finally said to me that she didn't need that kind of thing—she wanted more than just that. And I remember, it was like a cry of hers.

I think it's strange to be interested in young women. I think that it's a sign of something. My mother-in-law, Berdie, had a sister who wore three little spit curls stuck to her forehead. She started them at thirteen and had them at seventy. Now there is something weird about that, and I think that hanging on to attitudes is almost as weird. I am beginning to feel like what those curls looked like on this woman. It's just like habit— the one I finally yearn for is always somebody young. I don't know why.

There are guys who are attracted to younger women and don't do a fucking thing about it; there are guys who are attracted to younger women who go out and go up to Forty-second Street and they're at it all day long. Then there's someone who paints and he finds himself with some younger woman and she becomes his girl friend, and it's romance and they grow up together. But when somebody makes a capital case saying that all I've been doing my whole life is sitting around swimming pools and thinking about young women, what the hell do they mean? It's so foolish.

I'm not saying I'm not attracted to younger women. One of the nicest essays I read on *Lolita* was Lionel Trilling's. He calls it the greatest romance of our age because of the fantasy involved, the impossibility, the unreality.

Snow Cap, 1970

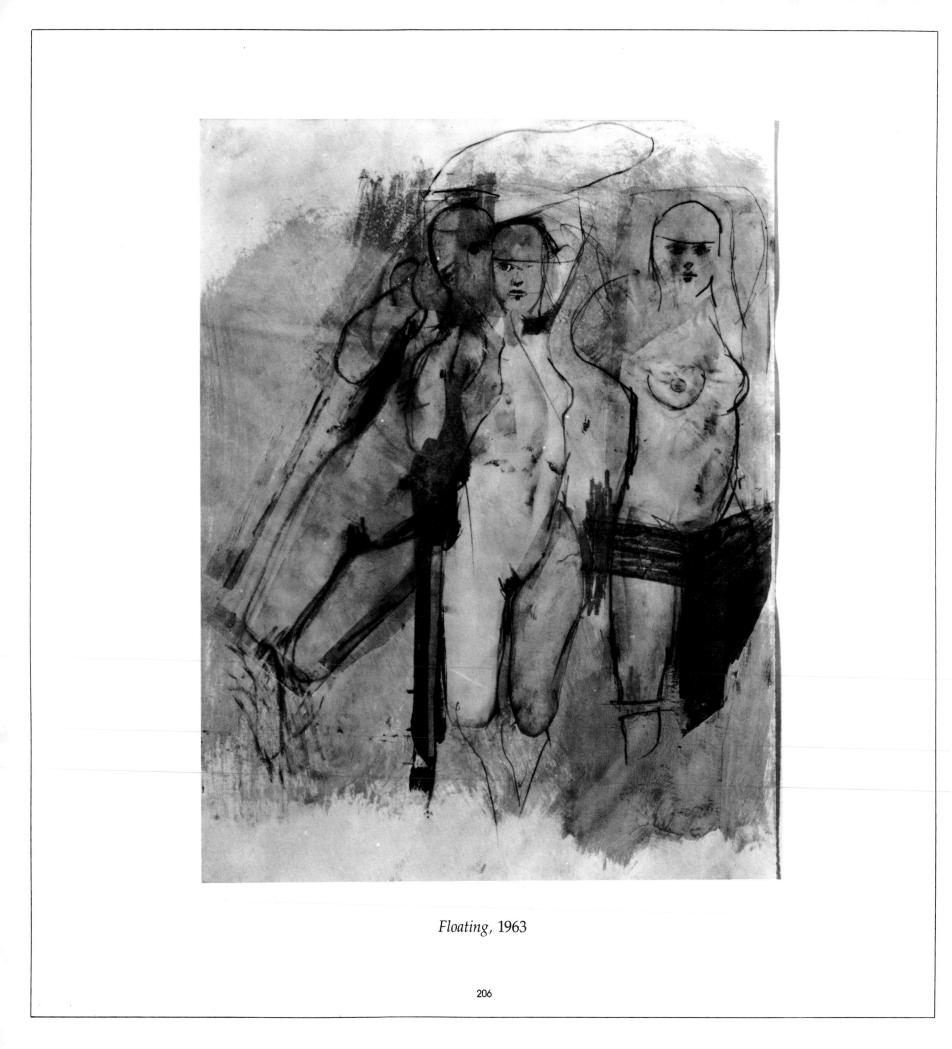

Floating, 1963

Monique's Dream, c.1966

Now we're looking at a later portrait of John Ashbery, who by this time has fallen under the knife. I may have done this drawing earlier on silver paper, and then as I grew to be less and less fond of it, I get rid of more and more of the peripheral. I cut just that part of the drawing that has some action, remove it from its original matrix, and then place it on a silver background. I would make a drawing and then make a line around the drawing.

Portrait of John Ashbery, c.1960

Spirit of Chicago, 1968

There's Carol, a portrait of Carol Selle. She's a rather brilliant drawing scholar, a collector and connected to the Museum of Modern Art and The Chicago Art Institute. Aside from what she looked like, I wanted to get something more about her in this work—an idea of her as a person who lived in Chicago, got into a plane every so often, came to New York, and had to keep resetting her watch.

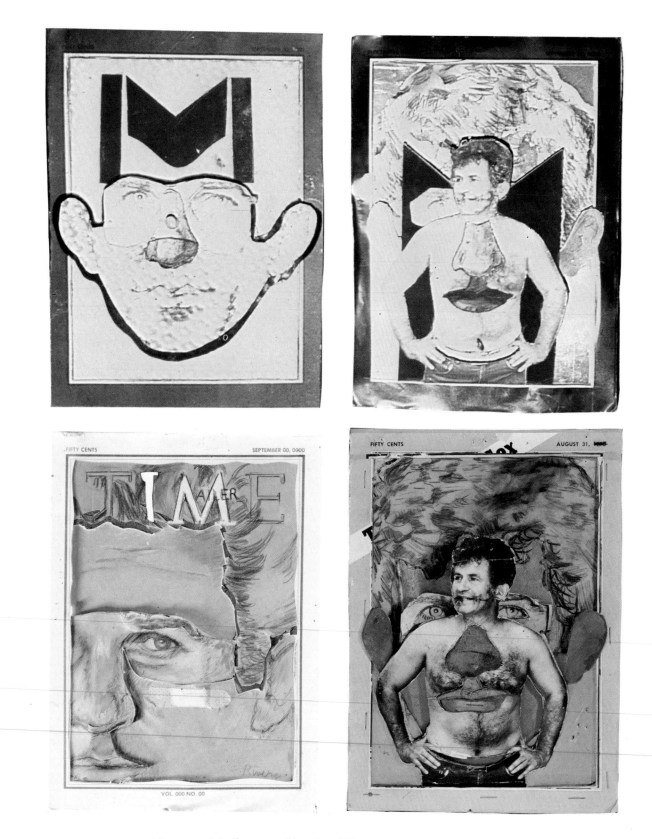

Norman Mailer, studies for *Time* magazine cover, 1968

This was commissioned by *Time* magazine for the cover—and I tried to do Macho Mailer, I guess.

Newsweek came out with Norman that same week or the week before, and it was cancelled. This would have been, I think, a pretty great cover. . . . I did a lot of cutting in my work at that time, and I did a lot of fitting; I became much more sculptural.

When was it—'68? He called me up and said, "Don't do it! Don't do it, Larry! I don't like them, they did this and that," and I said, "They're gonna do *something* of you, Norman, and it may as well be something that's good." But he's always been a fan of mine. I see him at parties sometimes. We're not friends, really—not at all. But I've known him a very long time. We were closer when we were younger. But given my own fairly developed ego, he makes me seem like a passive wallflower. I mean he's so *animated*.

Portrait of Aladar as a Hollow Column, 1971

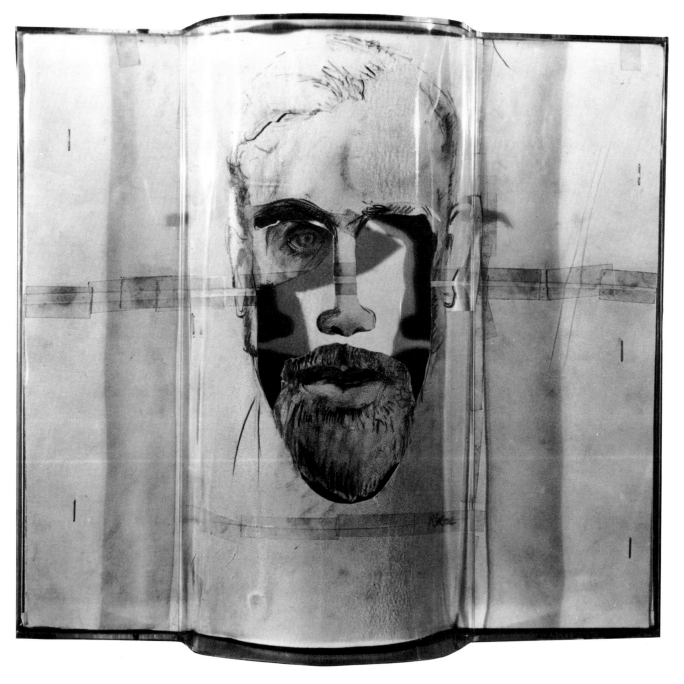

Head of Leonard Bernstein, 1965

That is Leonard Bernstein. I met Lenny through a girl named Ellen Oppenheim who had the closest thing to a literary/artistic salon in the fifties and sixties. When she was younger she lived with a composer in Europe who knew lots of intellectuals, and so she grew up in that kind of milieu. She's from a very illustrious Yiddish acting family, the Adlers. Her mother—Stella Adler—actually made it in Hollywood. When Ellen came back to New York she tried to reestablish the kind of milieu she was used to, and she did have writers and all sorts of people around. I met Lenny through her and then he and I became attracted to each other. I don't know why. I think maybe he had an erroneous notion of what kind of artist I was, and I had an erroneous notion of what kind of musical genius he was. Who knows?

He's very warm; sometimes it's almost automatic. I mean he's so warm so often you begin to wonder how warm he is. He is one of these people who puts his hand around you, looks you deep in the eyes, and says, "How ya been? How've you *really* been?"

On one of the days when he came over to Southampton from his summer house in Connecticut, I did this drawing. I have music paper around and I decided to do it on that. Very obvious, corny. And it really looks like him. It was just a quick thing again; I think most of my drawings of faces start like this. We talk for an hour or two and at the end of it I have actually done something. I'm too nervous to just sit around and waste time.

Lenny and I kept up for a while, we're sentimental about our past. Sometimes when I'm riding in the car and suddenly I hear Lenny Bernstein playing some concerto, I'm thrilled. He's a genius. He's this funny combination, a man steeped in the old masters and yet one who can write popular Broadway musicals. . . . I just saw him recently on the highway coming down from the Hamptons. In a car. We waved.

Template, Horse, Butterflies, Birds, 1965

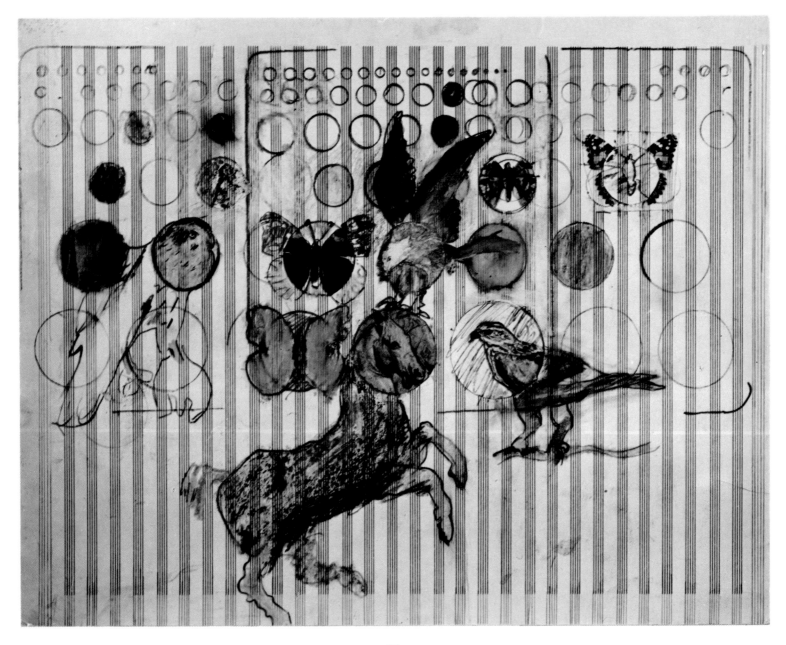

Nigeria's Africa, 1968

ELEVEN

AFRICA

Africa. It's very pop. You have to go there. They have themselves photographed with spears in front of a 747. Even *they* see how peculiar it is. You look for the Africa you saw in movies as a kid, and you go to places and run into that. You see people standing around, dancing to the music and you think, that's Africa. And then a freight train passes right through the village. The movie I did with Pierre Gaisseau was about all those juxtapositions of the primitive and the modern. Somebody was wearing some insane bone through his nose, and then some other guy would put a Kodak film can through his earlobe. They pick up on anything.

When I go to India or Africa, I take video equipment because I can't paint. And then it's fun. Maybe it's a dream, like every artist has a dream project in mind that he never really gets around to. There were a few years there when I was doing video and I did some films. Not that I wanted to stop painting, but I found that there was a real pull. Now I keep having this feeling that I'd really like to go and do another video-tape, but I've got to finish some painting, you see. I'm hung up on painting. I gotta do it or something's wrong. Let's say I don't feel completely sure of myself in painting, or I feel that there's art within me that will finally show how great a painter I am. It hasn't come out yet, and I think, "This is really gonna show 'em—this is gonna be fantastic! Then I won't have to do anything else." Somewhere there's that vaudevillian notion of an artist—the one who's going to be the greatest, see? I keep being compelled by that. And I think I'll finally get to the point where I'll really be able to say, OK, I'm not going to do *anything* for a month. But I keep getting involved in situations: somebody *commissions* a painting—I paint it. But in my mind my romance is with video. If the choice were there, I'd wake up and do that. I feel as if that was a genre that I really enjoyed, and I did some good things.

Patriotic Stamps I, 1976

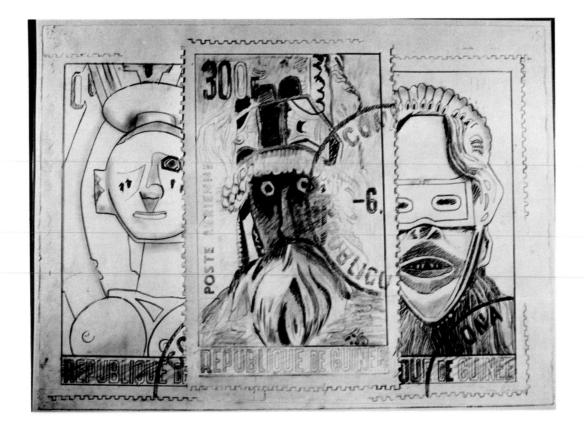

Patriotic Stamps III, 1976

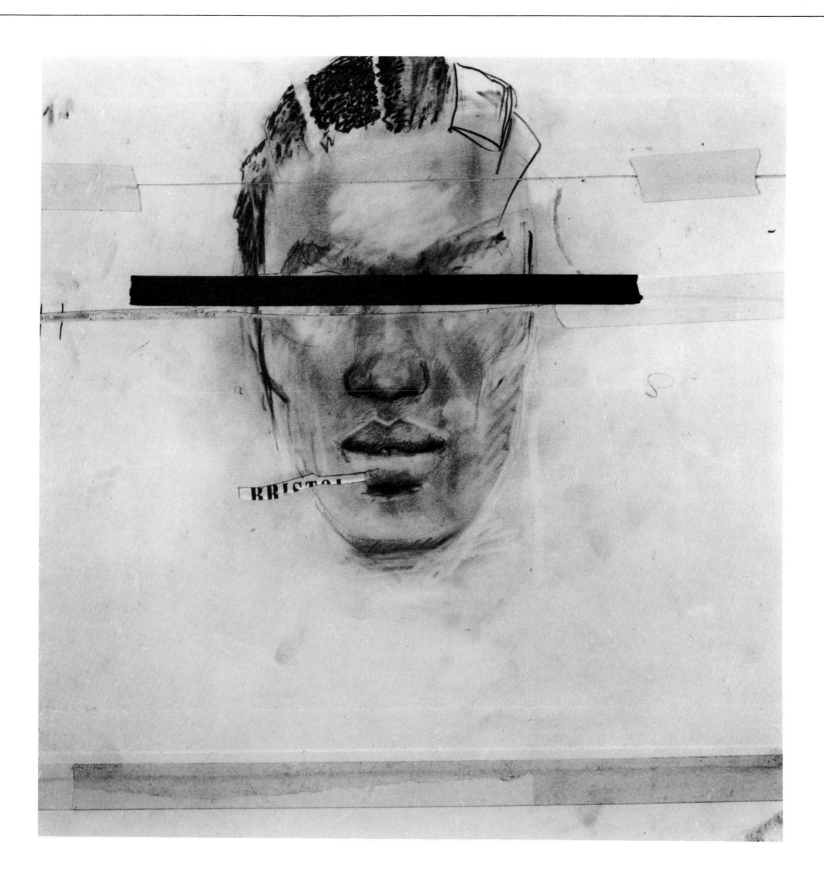

Zainipu, 1968

A girl friend of mine in Africa. When I came to Kenya
she stayed with me. She was a prostitute, but she
thought of herself as a terrific business lady.

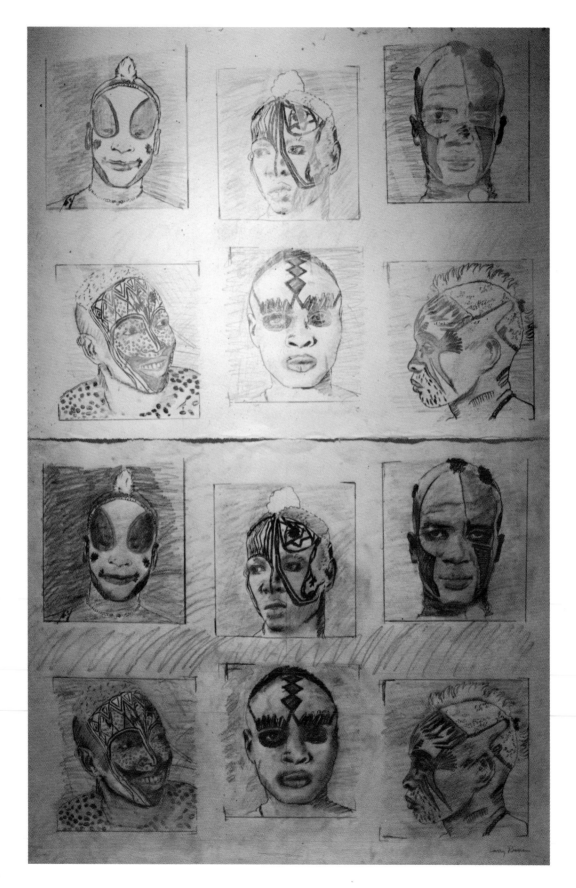

Leni's Kau People Carbon Color, 1976

Amboseli Elephants, 1968

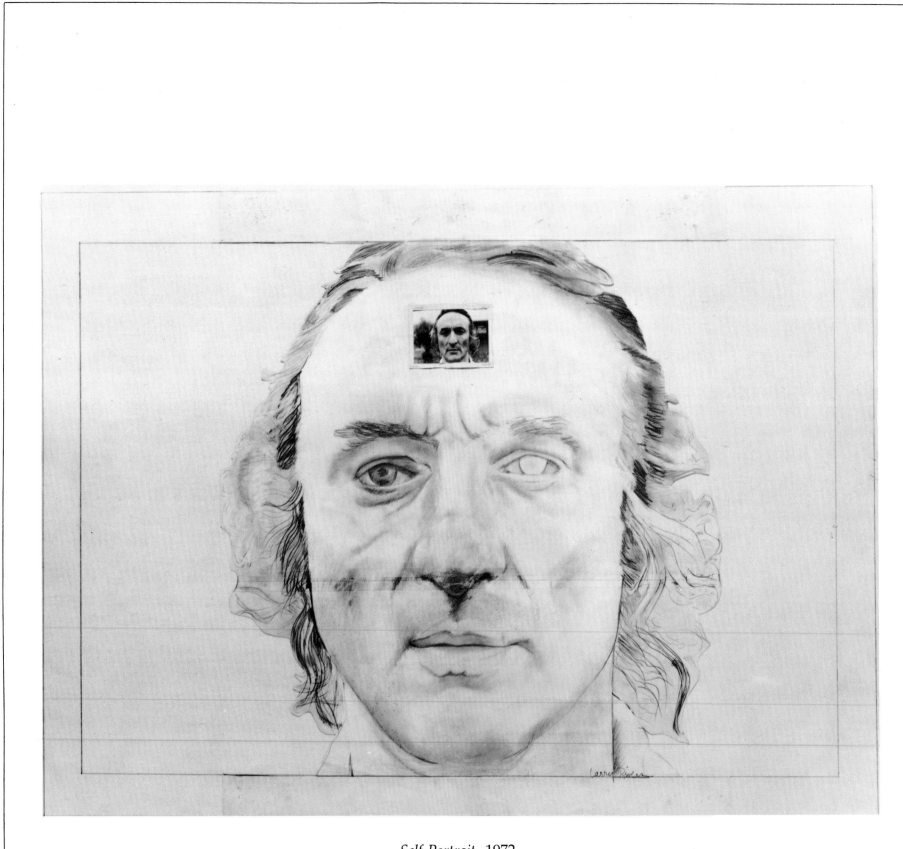

Self-Portrait, 1972

COMMISSIONS AND THE SEVENTIES

There used to be certain people's opinions I trusted to help show me what I was trying to do. Frank O'Hara was one person. But that doesn't seem to exist anymore for me. And it's difficult. I don't have any "mentor," so to speak. Tom Hess had a certain effect on me, but he didn't spend enough time with me—he couldn't help it. When people were younger and out of the world—I mean, their success wasn't part of their life yet—they could spend time with other people and think about other people. Now everybody's hung up on themselves.

So you're finally alone. That's really what it amounts to. Of course, in my case where I have an assistant, a guy who works with me like Rainer, I have an opinion daily. I mean the guy's there and watching me work, but it's part of his relationship to me. You can't take that as serious criticism. And also he's a painter himself, so it's something else. There are still a few people who take the time—Howard Kanovitz, Alex Katz. But mostly it's just listening to dealers or critics—you know, people who've got to write something; so really, you don't have anybody saying anything that sets you thinking. That's why I wonder where I am going to be replenished from. Myself constantly? I'm boring. It's hard to think that it could all come from yourself. I think, well, if I go out and look at art, I'll get some feedback from art. But I don't seem to. I don't seem to go out and look. So where will I be fed from? Maybe that is one of my weaknesses, and I was thinking that maybe there's a certain limitation in art when it's always the *self*. It happens to writers—I mean even some of *them* have gotten on your nerves, haven't they? Because it all seems to be about them. Are they taking a look at the world anymore? And you're bored.

I had this portrait tacked up on the wall and Earl McGrath came in and said, "Hey, that's nice, I'll give you fifty dollars for it and not a penny more." Every time he came over he'd go through that routine. "Hey, Larry. I'd like to buy that. I'll give you one hundred dollars for it and not a penny more." He'd go fifty dollars more every time. Finally, after about two years he was up to $1,800 and I said, "Sold," and now it's hanging on his wall.

These are drawings of a model, Evelyn Kuhn, commissioned by Harry Horn, a man who owns a sisal plantation outside Nairobi. He didn't know her; he came across her picture in a magazine and fell in love with her face. He was like an old-fashioned stage-door Johnny. He followed her career in magazines and on TV. Finally through my friend Peter Beard, Harry flew me to Africa to be seduced into the idea of doing a portrait from the photographs he had of her. He's a very generous man. I did two drawings; later I found out Avedon had done a portrait, so had the English painter, Alan Jones, and Harry had also commissioned one by Andy Warhol.

I thought Harry and Evelyn should never be allowed to meet. I mean, what reality can live up to that kind of fantasy? He did finally meet her in New York, along with her husband. End of story.

Beauty and the Beasts II, 1975

Beauty and the Beasts I, 1975

Good God! This is beautiful. How much better it is than the painting.

This is a drawing with a rather interesting history. It was commissioned by Lenny Holzer, an intellectual, a "well-known bachelor-around-town," the husband of Baby Jane. *Miss Oregon I* is a girl named Julie. She was a gorgeous girl and Lenny still mourns her death. He keeps this and he doesn't let anybody look at it. My work has produced the weirdest things. I sold him the painting, but he didn't pay me for about two years, so I just sold it to someone else, and he had to buy it back. He had a great sentimentality about this girl. She was in a few films. She was a kind of "marry me and take me away from all the problems of life" girl. But somehow, he wasn't divorcing his wife.

After she broke up with him she came to live right near me and we finally got around to a fantasy that I had about her for years—which probably one out of every two men who saw her had. But she was rather disturbed. She was all of twenty-one when she moved back to the Coast, and she died at twenty-two. She died in a fire.

This work is about ten feet wide. Over life-size. It was a work that grew in pieces. It was the most peculiar drawing when you think of how drawings are usually made. The arms themselves are four feet long. Making a line that you extend that far is not the same thing as taking a pencil and doing a sketch. A different technique takes place when you do these enormous drawings. You are using a pencil to create an image and people call it a drawing because pencils make drawings, but there should be some other name for it.

Portrait of Miss Oregon I, 1973

Divas: Maria Callas, Elizabeth Schwartzkopf, Leontyne Price, Victoria de las Angeles, c. 1962.

Look at her arms holding up her dress—the kind of dress that has many folds. A year later I went into Japanese work. All things add up.

I've done a lot of these portraits. It's funny, they are commissioned by men who are in love with these women. And I do it, I don't know why. And so again, Ad Reinhardt must be turning around in his grave.

She posed for the photograph all day. And then when I wanted to do her face, it took a few more days.

These portraits of the Johnson family were not commissioned at all. I knew them and I just decided I would like to try to do some drawings. After I did them they bought one or two of the works. *Summer Pregnancy* is one I kept. When the child was born, I put a drawing of the child in the larger drawing.

I like the Johnsons. They're Johnson & Johnson, a big corporation, and when you meet families like this and become friendly, families who hold a certain position in the world, it's peculiar. They are the princes of our time. The same with François deMenil. There's

She lent herself to this sexy pose. I inspired it—my brain, right? She gave in to men's notions of her, I guess. And she did have a beautiful figure, she did have a beautiful face. She was from Eugene, Oregon. She's like Miss Americana. Open eyes. . . . She could be exasperating and selfish and petty, you know, like everybody. She became an Arica person finally—you know those people? That was the finish.

something you can't escape. Someone has $200 million—that's charming!

The same with Jimmy Johnson. There's some aura that exists and it would be silly to deny it. On the other hand, a lot of artists get angry at it and reject it and say it doesn't mean anything. And when you analyze it, it doesn't really mean that much. But somehow you're still attracted to it.

I think that if you examine all art—except the primitive arts—you see it always takes place in societies where there is a lot of leisure.

Go Go and Camels, 1978

That's GoGo and Esther, her grandmother. Esther's quite a beautiful woman—just turned seventy. You know me, I leave out a few lines and they're eternally beautiful, eternally youthful. But I think it's a nice work.

She herself has a flair for dressing. I saw her in an elevator one day before I knew who she was, and she looked very interesting and fashionable to me. And then I got to know her. A year later when she finally decided that she'd pose for me, I made her wear one of her outfits. Now I think that underneath all these fashionable, contemporary, and stylish-looking clothes, there is a woman who's a kind of grandma. But I see her more as someone separate from the family, making her own existence and trying to carry on and be attractive and interesting. And she's got something. We have actually established a friendship on our own; we're in touch with each other over the phone—she's sympathetic about a lot of my weaknesses in the female department, and we talk.

Esther Johnson Dressed Up, 1978

Summer Pregnancy is from the carbon-paper syndrome. I translated this drawing into a painting and ended up with things happening in there that I never intended. There's some kind of aura.

The drawing part is more blocks of color really; but there are still details if you look, and there are realistic elements. It doesn't seem to be as rough, let's say, or as linear as the earlier drawings. There seems to be much more of a dense impact; like the colors are coming at you all at once. The bands of color and the little details that you can suddenly pick up in an easy way with tracing and projection.

Summer Pregnancy, 1977

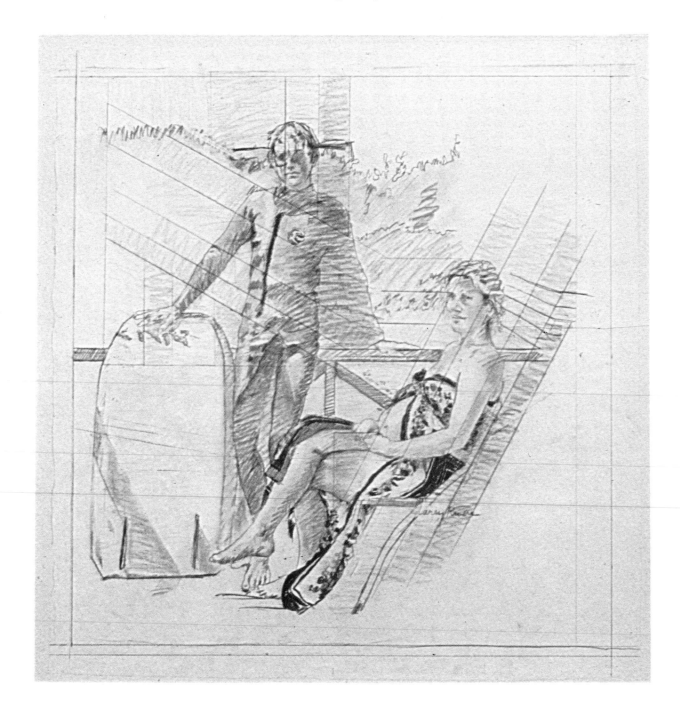

Tryout for Boston Massacre II, 1970

This was a bank commission and I had some idea that bankers are stiff, conservative people, but the man who commissioned it was a very nice man whom I got to know. According to our contract, he was allowed to come four times to see the progress of the work. We got along perfectly.

He used to write long letters in between visits about some things he wasn't sure of. He couldn't understand why a horse was riderless, for example, and so I would explain to him why it was and what I thought was going on: in this case that one of the riders had gotten off his horse to urinate.

There were two paintings in the commission. One was the *Boston Massacre* and one was the *Revere Event.* You know Revere actually got caught about an hour after he went out? He parlayed everything into the best that was good for him. He was admired by Hawthorne. There was a portrait of him by Copley.

This work is from a drawing that Paul Revere took credit for. He was a real rascal. He stole the idea from a man called Pelham who did this *Boston Massacre* drawing. Revere may have changed some things, but Pelham did the creative work before him, and Revere just got it out on the street first.

François and His Merlin, 1976

This is a drawing of François deMenil, who is a friend of mine. He had flown Michele Auder and me to Florida in his airplane, and I took the photograph for the drawing at the airport. It was some trip.

François commissioned this family portrait in 1975. He gave me a box of photographs and I chose about fifty that portrayed the family as a family where there are still children at home and parents who are thought of as parents, rearing children: I took the father when he was in his forties, I used a portrait of the mother when she was a bride, photographs of outings; I even used works of art that they own and put them in the drawing; Magrittes and Ernsts. So I covered a whole period and called the portrait *Family Album*.

Family Album, 1976

Two Lines of the Depression, 1975

The Stripe Is in the Eye of the Beholder: Portrait of Barnett Newman, 1975

May, 1968: Student Manifestation, 1979

May, 1968: Gaullist, 1979

May, 1968: Cohn-Bendit, 1979

May, 1968: Students and Police, 1979

May, 1968: Large C and 2½ Figures, 1979

Family photograph: artist's cousin's wedding photo taken in 1938

Social Patterns (Apart), 1979

Social Patterns (Together), 1979

Poem and Portrait of John Ashbery, 1977

THIRTEEN

PROJECTIONS, TRACINGS, AND CARBONS

I am by sheer accident, like you are your mother's daughter, a friend of John Ashbery, the poet. I mean we are good friends. I wanted to make a portrait of John and to do John Ashbery without a poem seemed to be a dumb thing. But to do it with a poem—that's something else. I connect it with the Renaissance where you'd have a naval captain and above his head the battle in which he'd won fame, a portrait of his face, God-given, and his venture on earth as a member of society. And John Ashbery, my friend, a very peculiar, marvelous person who could probably write a history of the French canal system just as well as he can write these marvelous poems.

It took my assistant three days with a projector to copy that poem—"Pyrography." He did such a lousy job that I had to go over it. There are 4,560-odd letters there. I had to go over every one. It took about a week. This is a work which is almost completely a product of mechanical devices. Here's how it goes.

I make a whole abstract arrangement of color carbons and tape them together. I put this arrangement of carbons down on a piece of paper. On another piece on top I draw a line—as it goes through yellow, blue, green, red country that line becomes yellow, blue, green, red. OK. I make a whole drawing like that. How can I translate that into a painting? I separate it. I see where the red part is. I interpolate it, blow it up to size in a different proportion, and I make a whole canvas with these color divisions. See that head in the blue field? I'm going to take that drawing from there, make a stencil of it, transpose it to the blue field on the canvas, take my brush, start working. That's one way.

I have another way of doing it. I take this whole thing, ignore the divisions first, make a realistic painting of John Ashbery from this photograph of him. Then later, over the realistic, naturalistic colors, I impose the blue, yellow, and red with airbrush like I do in the *Rembrandt* painting.

I like this way of working. It doesn't become a painting until you've filled it all in. You're filling, filling, filling, then finally it gets to the edge—it's there. Then you begin to do the kinds of things you do in the other kind of work. It gives me less anxiety. Before there were so many changes. Now I more or less know. Lots of people don't like it. It's funny, I don't know if you can go back. The other way had

Portrait of John Ashbery, 1977

certain fantastic qualities, I guess, and I don't know why I lost my nerve to just *begin painting*, but to get that table that way, to get the sense of the typewriter on the table right—I am interested in getting that right. Why should I have to struggle?"

Actually, it's been a long time since I worked directly without these mechanical devices. *The History of the Russian Revolution* was the last major work to include free line drawing and brushwork and that was in 1965. I am drawn, I think, by some ancient longing in man to have an objective way of reproducing a figure.

Do you know that etching by Dürer where an artist is shown viewing a seated figure through a pane of glass divided into squares? It's a good example of what I mean. The squares correspond to squares on a piece of graph paper and the figure is broken into parts and reassembled in the drawing, part by part, to achieve an "objective" representation. It's how I proceed now and it gives me a different feeling to work this way.

People sometimes say that the drawings of the fifties and sixties with all their erasures and smudges, and the psychological interest of the portraits, have more emotional impact than these later tracings. What led to the change? I think first that my interests were different then. When I drew and tried to get what your face looked like, I erased because I didn't like what I got. I smudged because I wanted to get the dark here and there. And so finally what comes out to the observer is something other than just my intention to get a kind of resemblance. It becomes the impact of the pencil movement, the color, the smudges, the erasures.

Now by the time I get to where I'm doing tracings, projections, carbons, my interests are no longer that kind of thing. I wanted another kind of impact from the work. And then the boredom thing comes in, too. I mean, how many years can you just smudge and erase? Who are you fooling? What are you trying to do? You're interested in products—I mean, the "Larry Rivers" product. I begin to be known as the guy who erases, smudges, and pushes this around; I keep going with it, even though I'm no longer doing it for the original reasons. And so you keep changing your interests; the pressures are on you to produce something you are interested in. What you go through to get this particular effect, say, with tracings and carbons, at least has a certain kind of freshness and validity and honesty.

Scale drawing for *Rainbow Rembrandt,* 1977

I think that lots of things that I've done in my work can be seen to originate in certain ways from my drawing. With Rembrandt's *Polish Rider*, I used airbrush rays to illuminate it. It looks like it's bathed in gels—a theatrical production. Insane. I think it's the most peculiar painting I've ever done. It's magical. The whole painting—except for the naturalism that is inherent in the touch—came out of the drawing: the whole division of the character into parts. The drawing leads these works. First I do a series of small sketches, then a large one. It's very hard. The guy has fifty objects on him: there's an ax, there are arrows, there's a bow, there's a knife, there's a big sword. It's crazy. I can't do it without a projection to go by. I don't go direct anymore—*at all*.

Carbon Color Drawing, Rainbow Rembrandt, 1977

Rainbow Rembrandt I, 1977

Kinko, the Nymph, Bringing Happy Tidings, 1974

I saw a book called *The Coloring Book of Japan*. The coloring books have gotten very sophisticated over the years, and here was this elaborate and arty thing on classic Japanese art. Being in black and white, you could see the structure of these famous Japanese paintings without the color. And for some reason that made me enjoy them in a way that I hadn't up till then. I like Japanese works, I knew Van Gogh was influenced by them, but for some reason they hadn't come across to me. Maybe the colors are too dead by the time you see them in reproductions or prints and they just don't have any juice. But in this book just

the structure was there, and it interested me and I began using it as the basis of this work.

I couldn't find the originals of any of these things so I fantasized the color myself. But structurally speaking they are exact copies of the coloring book, with just a very few alterations—things I thought weren't clear. And I thought it would be funny from an artistic point of view to add a few other things not found in Japanese painting, like heavy shadowing, which they don't use at all. Maybe artists will get it; I don't know if other people will.

Standing on a Libretto, 1974

Utamaro's Courtesans, 1974

This is called *The Resurrection of Tamara de Lempicka*. Tamara de Lempicka was a female who painted in Paris in the twenties and thirties; she migrated from Poland and she was from the aristocracy. She is now the Baroness Kuffner and living in Houston.

A few years ago I was walking along the rue St. Denis in Paris with a friend. It's a hookers' street, and it was very nice, very beautiful. And then we noticed this gallery and we went in to see the exhibition which was of her work. I brought back the poster of her original painting from Paris and hung it up on the wall and kept it there for three years. There was something about its cubist, futuristic look that I liked—she really is quite an interesting painter. Tamara de Lempicka seemed to have brought S & M into her work; there were ladies in boots with purple hair, and she made a portrait of herself in an automobile with a sort of headpiece flying back in the wind. She was quite thrilling from the subject-matter point of view. It's funny that I chose this one, the mandolinist; it's more central to her kind of work, but now I regret that I didn't do the one in the boots.

Resurrecting Tamara de Lempicka, 1977

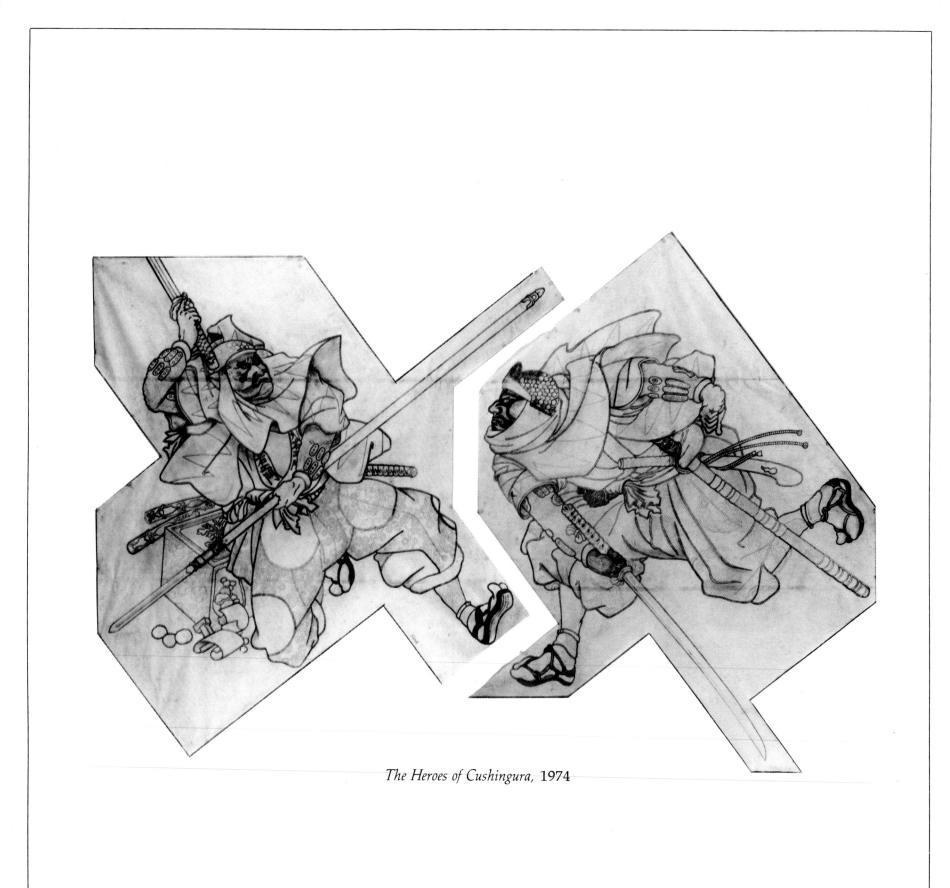

The Heroes of Cushingura, 1974

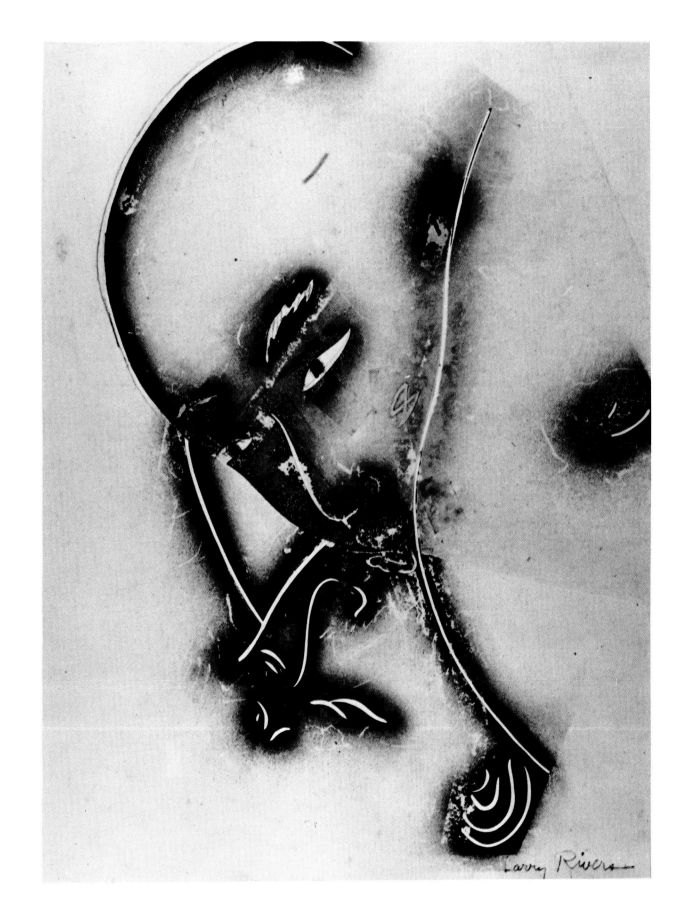

The Kiss: Japanese Erotic Art Stencil, 1974

FOURTEEN

THE GOLDEN OLDIES

So many painters I knew just kept working on the same thing for twenty-five years. They don't seem to change that much. And so I'm thinking to myself, I'm not really doing anything that original with *The Golden Oldies*. I just decided that some of these subjects have elements that I continue to like. There really is some kind of development. There's a particular suit that Napoleon is wearing, and it's always interested me. I find that I like to deal with that kind of cream-white-yellow. And then there's also the repetition of forms and change; from one version to the next you sort of drop certain things that appeared in the first version and pick up on other things in the second version.

In the end I chose those works from my past which I think are popular—like "golden oldies" records that sell more than a million. I chose those works which I thought identified me in a public sense—*The Greatest Homosexual*, which made a big splash at the time, or the *French Vocabulary Lesson* and the *Camels*. On the other hand, I also chose works that weren't known very well, like some of the drawings. If you missed it the first time around, now you can see them all on one surface.

I'm interested in history and I've done paintings based on history. I'm beginning to have my own history that's getting so thick that I can begin to almost deal with it alone as a subject. I'm accepting this idea that I'm some kind of historical fact. Peculiar. I am and I'm not. We all are.

But all the time, I'm wondering what I'll do when I get back to real art—as if I'm going to take up the thread at this point. You ask me if I've been putting off that question. I don't know. I've always thought that one has to deal with fresh material. You experiment, you don't stick with anything that becomes rote. That's not art. I mean, how could I now come back to this so easily? To the old stuff? I should move on and keep experimenting . . . but I'm trying to think—maybe I haven't. Then the other kind of Picasso personality is open to criticism, too—I mean now, for me. Why? Because I think that you don't get that far away from yourself anyway.

For myself there must be that other route which is where your affections take you, and where you keep working out the little kinks and all that. I think that what has happened is that I've decided that there is a certain framework and that I need to operate within it. Obviously I'm enjoying the old images and I'm familiar with them. They become your own world. . . .

But then look what happens. Jean Tinguely got in touch with me while I was working on the *Golden Oldies*, and said he was thinking of *The History of the Russian Revolution*. Here it is fifteen years later, and he wants to do something three-dimensional. So I figured something out: I'm going to do a lot of drawing, and he's going to translate it into steel and use it in his huge construction outside Paris. I will make what I want in line, and he will heat and bend steel rods to execute it. It's going to be a long, fantastic piece. And it's funny—I was going to do a sixties piece next anyway and I was going to have three-dimensional elements in the next one. By the time I come back from France I will already have the feel of three-dimensional. So isn't life funny? I'm interrupting the process of this work, *The Golden Oldies*, to go work with a guy on something which was already in me. I mean, the artist puts everything to use.

Golden Oldies: Parts of the Body—Italian, 1978

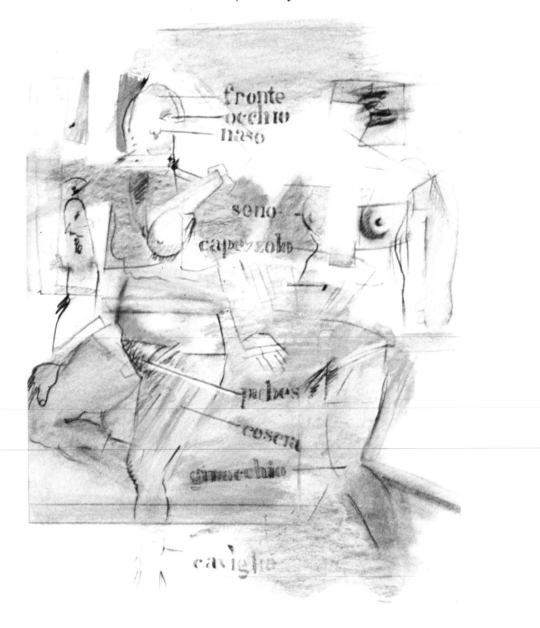

Golden Oldies: The Greatest Homosexual, 1978

Golden Oldies: French Money, 1978

Golden Oldies: French Money II, 1978

Golden Oldies: Bunch of Noses, 1978

Golden Oldies: Dying and Dead Veteran, 1978

I used to read newspapers all the time. I couldn't start my day without them. Now I don't read the *Times.* I find the *New York Times*, Jimmy Carter, the rest of the politicians and what they're trying to do, the movement of society—uninteresting. Then there's the *Village Voice*, which in some ways is much more "political" than, say, the *New York Times*; it takes sides in a very strong way and it's very culture-conscious. I mean it has pages and pages of reviews and talk about shows and musicals and art, and for some reason, I don't know why—I just can't read that newspaper. Is it some world that I don't want to face? Is it my generation? Or is it too much for me? I mean, what is it?

There are things happening in the theatrical world, there are things happening in the dance world, there are things happening in the art world, the poetry world, the music world—it's all there, right? Somehow. But I don't seem to be that interested. I seem to have faded out of culture so to speak. In the fifties and sixties I had a feeling I was in touch. I think I went every other night to the New York City Center, even if I showed up for the last dance. Maybe it was Frank O'Hara. I seemed to go to all sorts of literary parties, art parties. I don't seem to do that anymore.

On the other hand, the records show us that the amount of people going has increased yearly. People go to see more ballets than football games. There are some openings you can't get into. So maybe there's always been that curve of up and down in your own life, and you don't even realize it. But I suspect that people approach art today as consumers rather than in a more personal way. The whole country's changed.

Golden Oldies: Camels, 1978

Golden Oldies: Queen of Clubs, 1978

Golden Oldies:Rejected Copy, 1978

I am the kind of person who lets himself be moved by outside influences. I paint and draw on commission. I do prints. I am that kind of artist. But there is that other kind of artist like de Kooning who not only doesn't take commissions—he won't even do prints, he never does anything but what comes from himself; he doesn't respond to ideas other people have for his work. Maybe he's moved by things he's read and things he's seen—we're all pushed. Where does it all come from? It comes from experience. But a lot of my art comes from other people's desires. I have a social personality.

You can have five million ideas in painting. I had the carbon-copy idea. I had the whole thing worked out. I put a piece of carbon paper down; I make the line. It's exactly what I said I was going to do, and I take a look at it and *I don't like it*. Now where am I?

What is all this talk about making money, drugs, sex, everything else? There is the moment where you're really left bare, naked—with just the things you know about art, about craft. What are you going to do? You may be a fool in life as all of us are, and then for a certain existential moment—not a heroic moment—none of this does anything for you; none of your thoughts, none of the books written about you, the museums you're in—nothing. You suddenly reach into yourself, you make a decision. Red? Blue? Line? Bring it in? Bring in something else? Should I tear it up? Make it bigger? Somehow you reach into yourself, pull out something and try to do something with it.

You ask what in my work I would think important and hold on to, what I would let go? It's a long story. I just found a piece that I didn't look at for eight years, and I like it very much. Every so often I find a neglected work that no one liked, and suddenly it's like a child in the family who isn't as good-looking but has certain qualities that you admire. I don't know. What would I let go? There are certain things that I've done that show me more about my character that I'd let go. A person once told me what a wonderful drawing they saw of mine, and they wondered if I had anything like that around. I actually made it that day, and then I showed it to them as if I had done it ten years ago. So I would say I wouldn't hold on to that one.

But like what is the whole thing about, you ask—what have I done? This week I think maybe I didn't do anything. I don't know. I just think I have a certain amount of energy, and I work and people seem to want it; people are attracted from time to time and I'm prey to that, I respond to that, like people do. It's also an attempt to continue an identity: I'm Larry Rivers, the artist; if I stopped tomorrow would I still be Larry Rivers, the artist? But I keep thinking that I want to continue this identity and so I work, and this week it feels sort of foolish.

I'm still in a very bad mood and I don't know exactly what it is. I seem to be dealing more with my career than with actual work. You've got to have a career because you've done work, then the career becomes something else to do with museums, collectors, shows, books, and the work becomes just one part of this whole big picture, and suddenly in this particular period, I don't seem to be doing any work. I guess I shouldn't worry. I mean, I've done a lot of things and if I stop today what I've done resembles a respectable output—and I always keep thinking I'm going to do one more great one, you know, like everybody else. But it feels peculiar. I think that a lot of it has to do with the fact that I devoted a year to the *Golden Oldies*, and it's now beginning to dawn on me that after going back and looking at the works in my past, now I have to turn around the other way and look at what's ahead. And what do I see out there in front of me? What am I going to do?

If I look at Picasso's later years I think to myself: well, it's great that he did what he did. I am glad he worked till ninety-one. But given what we know of Picasso, he was probably finished when he was what? Fifty, sixty. So you can take your choice. But what are you going to do with yourself? I don't say Picasso should have stopped. What I'm trying to say is that a man keeps working because there probably is nothing else to do that interests him as much. Maybe painting is an old man's art. Almost everything else gets more and more difficult as you get older; your work stands for something.

Golden Oldies, 60s, 1978

164A *Xerox Drawing of "Oil" McGrath*, 1968
Xerox with pencil on paper, 16 ½ x 21 ¼"
Collection of Earl McGrath, New York

164B *Portrait of Taylor*, 1966
Pencil on paper, 14 ¼ x 16 ⅞"
Marlborough Gallery, New York

165 *Tex, Portrait of Terry Southern*, 1971
Pencil on paper, 18 x 21"
Collection of Terry Southern

166 *How to Draw Horses*, 1961
Pencil on paper, 17 x 14"
Collection of Fernando Zóbel de Ayala, Cuenca, Spain

167 *Kiki*, 1965–66
Medical rubber stamps, colored pencil on paper, 22 x 30"
Collection of Kiki Kogelnik

168A *Camels*, 1962
Pencil on paper, 14 ½ x 13"
Gimpel Fils Gallery Ltd., London

168B *Camel Drawing*, 1962
Pencil on paper, 16 x 14"
Marlborough Gallery, New York

169 *French Camel Carbon Paper*, 1976
Colored carbon on paper, 36 x 46 ½"
Collection of Mrs. Henry J. Kaiser

170 Fragment, *Head of Frank O'Hara*, 1954
Pencil on paper, 6 ⅛ x 5 ⅛"
The Museum of Modern Art, New York

172 *O'Hara Reading*, 1967
Color lithograph and collage, 27 ½ x 32 ¼"
Collection of Tatyana Grosman, Universal Limited Art Editions

173 *Frank and Poem*, illustration and poem "For the Chinese New Year and for Bill Berkson" from *In Memory of My Feelings*,
The Museum of Modern Art, 1969
Private Collection

174 *In Memory of the Dead*, 1967
Relief, spray paint, collage, 30 x 21"
Private Collection

175 *Don't Fall and Me*, 1966
Oil and collage on canvas, 16 ¼ x 28"
Private Collection

177 *Elimination of Nostalgia I*, 1967
Crayon and pencil relief on board, 12 x 9 ¼"
Collection of Dr. Mario L. Laurenti

178 *Henry Geldzahler*, 1964
Pencil and collage on graph paper, 16 ½ x 21 ½"
The Museum of Modern Art, New York
(The Joan and Lester Avnet Collection)

182A Actual Webster cigar-box label

182B *Carbon Webster*, 1962
Pencil and colored carbon on paper, 8 x 7 ½"
Private Collection

183 *Webster and Europe*, 1967
Relief collage with crayon and charcoal, 18 x 20"

The Phoenix Art Museum, Arizona
(Gift of Mr. Edward Jacobson)

185 *Portrait of Howard Kanovitz*, 1964
Pencil on paper, 11 x 13 ½"
Collection of Mr. and Mrs. David Reichart

186A *John Gruen in Plastic*, c. 1966
Pink Day-Glo paper on textured plastic, 11 ½ x 11 ½ x 4 ¾"
Collection of John Gruen

186B *Lions from the Dreyfus Fund*, c. 1966
Pencil and collage on paper
Private Collection

187 *Portrait of a Budding Art Historian*, 1968
Pencil, ball-point, Day-Glo paper, and collage, 18 x 24"
Collection of Rita Reif, New York

188 *No Name Portrait*, 1968
Pencil on paper, 14 x 17"
Collection of Mr. and Mrs. Nathan Whitman

189 *Lenin with Tie*, 1965
Collage with pencil, crayon, spray paint, and a tie, 20 ½ x 24"
Galerie Roger d'Amécourt, Paris

190A Rembrandt, *Syndics of the Drapers' Guild*, 1662
Oil on canvas, 75 ¼ x 110"
Rijksmuseum, Amsterdam

190B Actual Dutch Masters cigar-box label

191 *Golden Oldies: Dutch Masters*, 1978
Colored pencil, charcoal, and acrylic on paper, 89 x 57"
Jeffrey H. Loria Collection, New York

192A *Mauve Masters*, 1963
Oil and collage on board, 25 x 26"
Private Collection

192B *Dutch Masters VF*, 1963
Paper collage encased in plastic, mounted on wood, 7 ⅝ x 13 ¼"
Collection of Pamela Walker, Washington, D.C.

193A *Dutch Masters Silver*, 1968
Construction with pencil, crayon, and silver paper, 11 ¾ x 16"
Private Collection

193 *Dutch Masters*, drawing for banner, c. 1966
Pencil and collage on paper, 30 ¼ x 26 ¼"
Collection of Dr. Heinz Hunstein

194 *Silver Infanta*, 1962
Oil on paper with collage, mounted on board under Plexiglas, 26 ½ x 28 ½"
Collection of Mrs. Sue King

197 *Putting an Eye on It*, 1969
Collage with optical effects in Plexiglas box, 14 ¼ x 17 ¾"
Collection of the Artist

198 *Anemones*, 1963
Pencil and colored papers on board, 9 x 10"
Collection of Clarice Rivers

199A *Jim Dine Storm Window Portrait*, position 1: panel up, 1965
Mixed media, 29 x 25 x 2 ¾"
Collection of the Artist

199B Position 2: panel down

199C Position 3: panel switched

201 *Tinguely Storm Window Portrait*, position 2: panel down, (in collaboration with Niki de Saint Phalle), 1965
Oil and collage on board with storm window, 20 x 25 x 2 ¾"
Private Collection

202 *Miss Popcorn*, 1972
Acrylic on vinyl, 72 x 43"
Museo de Arte Contemporaneo, Caracas, Venezuela

203 *Reclining Models and Shoes*, 1966
Collage and mixed media, 15 ¾ x 20"
Collection, Dr. & Mrs. Martin L. Gecht, Chicago

205 *Snow Cap*, 1970
Paper collage with pencil and colored crayon, encased in plastic, 17 x 14"
Private Collection

206 *Floating*, c. 1963
Pencil and charcoal on paper
Private Collection

207 *Monique's Dream*, 1966
Canvas collage construction, 28 ¼ x 24 ¼"
Private Collection

208 *Portrait of John Ashbery*, c. 1960
Pencil on paper pasted on silver paper, 16 ½ x 14 ½"
Collection of John Ashbery

209 *Spirit of Chicago*, 1968
Pencil on gray paper with Day-Glo paper, 12 x 18"
Collection of Mr. & Mrs. Richard L. Selle

210A *Norman Mailer*, study for *Time* magazine cover, 1968
Collage relief, 11 ½ x 8 ½"
Collection of the Artist

210B *Norman Mailer*, study for *Time* magazine cover, 1968
Collage relief, 11 ½ x 8 ½"
Collection of the Artist

210C *Norman Mailer*, study for *Time* magazine cover, 1968
Collage relief, 11 ½ x 8 ½"
Collection of the Artist

210D *Norman Mailer*, study for *Time* magazine cover, 1968
Collage relief, 11 ½ x 8 ½"
Collection of the Artist

211 *Portrait of Aladar as a Hollow Column*, 1971
Pencil and tape on paper in plastic, 14 x 16"
Collection of Aladar Marberger

212 *Head of Leonard Bernstein*, 1965
Pencil on music paper, 14 x 16"
Collection of Leonard Bernstein

213 *Template, Horse, Butterflies, Birds*, 1965
Mixed media with collage on music paper, 14 ½ x 18"
Collection of James Rosenquist

214 *Nigeria's Africa*, 1968
Mixed media on paper, 10 ⅞ x 11 ¾"
Collection of the Artist

216A *Patriotic Stamps I*, 1976
Colored pencil on paper, 36 ⅝ x 25 ⅝"

Collection of the Artist

216B *Patriotic Stamps III*, 1976
Colored pencil with stencil on paper, 36 ⅝ x 25 ⅝"
Collection of the Artist

217 *Zainipu*, 1968
Pencil and collage on paper, 13 ⅜ x 14"
Albrecht Art Museum, St. Joseph, Mo.

218 *Leni's Kau People Carbon Color*, 1976
Colored carbon and colored pencil on paper, 78 ¼ x 50 ½"
Atlantic Richfield Company Art Collection

219 *Amboseli Elephants*, 1968
Pencil, spray paint, and raised cutouts, 36 x 26 x 5 ¼"
Private Collection

220 *Self-Portrait*, 1972
Pencil with Polaroid photograph, 39 ½ x 50"
Collection of Earl McGrath

222 *Beauty and the Beasts II*, 1975
Pencil on paper, 70 ¾ x 78 ½"
Collection of Harry Horn, Nairobi, Africa

223 *Beauty and the Beasts I*, 1975
Pencil on paper, 78 ½ x 70 ¾"
Private Collection

224 *Portrait of Miss Oregon I*, 1973
Mixed media on paper, 66 x 108"
Collection of Leonard Holzer

225 *Divas: Maria Callas, Elizabeth Schwartzkopf, Leontyne Price, Victoria de las Angeles*, c. 1962
Pencil on paper, 12 ½ x 19 ¼"
Private Collection

226 *Go Go and Camels*, 1978
Color pencil and acrylic on canvas, 60 x 40"
Private Collection, New Jersey

227 *Esther Johnson Dressed Up*, 1978
Colored pencil and acrylic on canvas, 24 x 18"
Private Collection, New Jersey

228 *Summer Pregnancy*, 1977
Colored pencil on paper, 36 x 34"
Collection of the Artist

229 *Study for Boston Massacre II*, 1970
Colored crayon, 30 x 40"
Commission for New England Merchant's National Bank of Boston
Private Collection

230 *François and His Merlin*, 1976
Mixed media on paper, 60 x 82"
Collection of François de Menil

231 *Family Album*, 1976
Mixed media on paper, 96 x 144"
Collection François de Menil

232 *Two Lines of the Depression*, 1975
Pencil and colored pencil on paper, 84 x 84"
Marlborough Gallery, New York

233 *The Stripe Is in the Eye of the Beholder: Portrait of Barnett Newman*, 1975
Pencil on paper, 35 ¾ x 100 ½"
Collection of Mr. David Pincus

Five of eight drawings commemorating the student uprisings in Paris, May, 1968 commissioned by Jean Tinguely, Niki de Saint Phalle and Rainer von Hessen

234A *May 1968: Student Manifestation,* 1979
Pencil and colored pencil on paper,
60 x 86"
Private Collection

234B *May, 1968: Gaullist,* 1979
Pencil and colored pencil on paper,
29 ½ x 42"
Private Collection

234C *May 1968: Cohn-Bendit,* 1979
Pencil and colored pencil on paper,
29 ½ x 48 ½"
Private Collection

234D *May, 1968 Students and Police,* 1979
Pencil and colored pencil on paper,
68 x 85"
Private Collection

235 *May, 1968 Large C and 2 ½ Figures,* 1979
Pencil and colored pencil on paper,
80 x 58"
Private Collection

236A Family photograph: artist's cousin's wedding photo taken in 1938

236B *Social Patterns (Apart),* 1979
Pencil on paper, 29 x 36 ½"
Collection of the Artist

237 *Social Patterns (Together),* 1979
Pencil on paper, 78 x 94"
Collection of the Artist

238 *Poem and Portrait of John Ashbery,* 1977
Pencil and colored carbon on
canvas, 76 x 58"
Collection of the Artist

240 *Portrait of John Ashbery,* 1977
Colored pencil on paper,
22 ½ x 30"
Robert Miller Gallery, New York

241 Scale drawing for *Rainbow
Rembrandt,* 1977
Pencil on colored carbon and

paper, 65 x 75 ½"
Collection of Joseph H. Hirshhorn

242 Color drawing for *Rainbow
Rembrandt,* 1977
Crayon and pencil on paper, 30 x 42"
Collection of Joseph H. Hirshhorn

243 *Rainbow Rembrandt I,* 1977
Acrylic on canvas, 66 x 76"
Collection of Joseph H. Hirshhorn

244 *Kinko, the Nymph, Bringing Happy
Tidings,* 1974
Pencil and colored pencil on paper,
78 x 108"
Collection of Kitty Meyers

245 *Standing on a Libretto,* 1974
Pencil and colored pencil on paper,
80 ¼ x 54"
Collection of Richard Himmel

246 *Utamaro's Courtesans,* 1974
Pencil and colored pencil on paper,
81 ½ x 70"
Collection of Kitty Meyers

247 *Resurrecting Tamara de Lempicka,* 1977
Acrylic on canvas, 50 x 32 ½"
Collection of Jennifer Gregg

248A Left-hand hero for *Heroes of
Cushingura,* 1974
Pencil and colored pencil on paper,
54 x 80 ½"
Collection of Kitty Meyers

248B Right-hand hero for *Heroes of
Cushingura,* 1974
Pencil and colored pencil on
tracing paper, 54 x 80 ½"
Collection of Kitty Meyers

249 *The Kiss: Japanese Erotic Art Stencil,* 1974
Acrylic and stencil paper, 24 x 17 ¾"
Collection of the Artist

250 *Golden Oldies, 50s,* 1978

Oil and mixed media on canvas,
106 x 144"
Private Collection, Fukuoka, Japan

252 *Golden Oldies: Parts of the Body—
Italian,* 1978
Pencil and pastel on paper, 24 x 18"
Private Collection, New York

253 *Golden Oldies: The Greatest Homosexual,*
1978
Colored pencils and acrylic on
vellum, 83 ¾ x 57 ½"
Private Collection, New York

254A *Golden Oldies: French Money I,* 1978
Colored pencils and mixed media
on paper, 37 ¼ x 61 ⅝"
Private Collection, New York

254B *Golden Oldies, French Money II,* 1978
Colored pencils, pastel, and acrylic
on paper, 34 x 58"
Private Collection, New York

255A *Golden Oldies: Bunch of Noses,* 1978
Pastel on colored paper,
18 ⅝ x 12 ⅞"
Private Collection, New York

255B *Golden Oldies: Dying and Dead Veteran,*
1978
Pencil and pastel on paper,
72 ½ x 59"
Collection of the Artist

256 *Golden Oldies: Camels,* 1978
Pencil and pastel on paper
Private Collection, New York

257 *Golden Oldies: Queen of Clubs,* 1978
Pencil, colored pencil, and pastel
on paper, 28 x 24"
Collection of the Artist

258 *Golden Oldies: Rejected Copy,* 1978
Pencil and pastel on paper, 29 x 24"
Collection of the Artist

260 *Golden Oldies, 60s,* 1978
Acrylic and mixed media on
canvas, 106 x 144"
Jeffrey H. Loria Collection, New York

P H O T O
C R E D I T S

The Art Institute of Chicago; pages 20,
36, 57, 78, 80, 91, 117B, 161
Rudolph Burckhardt; pages 41B, 192A
Pete Darling Studio; page 209
Detroit Art Institute; page 108
Jonas Dovydenas; pages 54A, 54B
Dwan Gallery; pages 107, 109
eeva-inkeri; pages 228, 238, 240–243, 247
John Gruen; page 123
Aida and Robert E. Mates; pages 25, 32,
33, 40, 47, 49A, 53, 89, 122, 128A, 128B,
129, 132, 139, 141, 160B, 162, 165, 186A,
191, 198, 220, 226, 227, 232, 250, 252,
253, 254A, 255A, 255B, 256, 258, 260
Robert E. Mates and Paul Katz; pages 224,
244, 246, 248A, 248B
The Metropolitan Museum of Art; pages
60, 93
Peter Moore; page 94
The Museum of Modern Art; pages 58,
60–69, 75, 76, 90, 93, 130A, 130B, 131A,
131B, 170, 178
O. E. Nelson; pages 29, 43, 56, 95, 118, 135,
147D, 156, 174, 182B, 188, 189, 197, 207,
214, 217, 229
Tony Rogers; page 160A
Thomas Rose; page 208
Steven Sloman; pages 98, 205
John F. Waggarman; pages 100, 102, 103

Dear Out There:

   The collection of drawings that appears here is in many ways based on luck—drawings that were photographed before they were sold, works whose history remains in my brain that could be traced, drawings in my own collection, whatever friends hung onto, etc. Suffice it to say I've done many more drawings than are reproduced in this volume. It seems likely that there will be a second edition, and out of both curiosity and a desire to produce a broader idea of my work, I (and the Publisher) would appreciate hearing from anyone who knows the whereabouts of other drawings of mine.

Larry Rivers, New York, 1979

Write: Larry Rivers, c/o Clarkson N. Potter, Inc., One Park Avenue, New York, N.Y. 10016

A   N O T E   O N   T H E   T Y P E

The text of this book was set in Palatino, designed in 1948 by the German typographer Hermann Zapf and issued between 1950 and 1952. Palatino is distinguished by its broad letters and vigorous, inclined serifs. Named after Giovanbattista Palatino, it was the first of Hermann Zapf's typefaces to be introduced to America.

The book was composed by Publishers Phototype Inc. in Carlstadt, New Jersey, and printed and bound by Toppan Printing Company (America) Inc. in Japan. The text was printed in Offset, the color plates in four-color process, and the black-and-white illustrations were printed in Duotone.

Edited by Carol Southern
Production editing by Pamela Pollack
Production supervision by Michael Fragnito and Elizabeth M. Ferranti
Designed by Hermann Strohbach

OD   3270S B

4/12/90

32705 B